THEO KALOMIRAKIS'

Private
THEATERS

THEO KALOMIRAKIS'
Private
THEATERS

By Brett Anderson
Photographed by Phillip H. Ennis

WITH AN INTRODUCTION BY
Roger Ebert

◆

Home Theater Magazine
Harry N. Abrams, Inc., Publishers

Library of Congress Catalog Card Number: 97–70382
ISBN 0–8109–6344–2

Copyright © 1997 CurtCo Freedom Group
Photographs © 1997 Phillip H. Ennis

Published in 1997 by *Home Theater Magazine*, a division of CurtCo Freedom Group,
    Malibu, California
Distributed in 1997 by Harry N. Abrams, Incorporated, New York

Printed and bound in Hong Kong

Harry N. Abrams, Inc.
100 Fifth Avenue
New York, N.Y. 10011
www.abramsbooks.com

ACKNOWLEDGEMENTS

No amount of words can express my gratitude to the following individuals for their assistance: my team of talented and dedicated associates, Gary Griggs, Yujin Asai, Alejandro Gonzalez, and Giuseppe Provenzano, for designing with me the theaters included in this book; Peter Avedon, Tony Bruzzesi, Brad Carlson, Joe Di Staulo, Gordon DeWitt, Bob Weinberg, Bob Eustic, Matt Kehoe, Frank Gallagher, Rick Nerdling, George Parker, and their hard-working crews who built the theaters; Bill Anderson, Eric Eidelman, Robert Eitel, Robert Kaufman, Brett Sandgren, Bob Serio, and Pierre Spenard who equipped them with state-of-the-art picture and sound; Bary Silverstein for his guidance and moral support during the difficult first years; Skip Bronson and Barbara Fabian for being my first clients and remaining my closest friends; Bruce Nelson, Neil Zuckerman, and Tom Shivers for giving me the first push in this business; Scott Carlson for believing in me and allowing me to concentrate on my custom-designed work; Alison Bluestone, Marc Franken, Martin McClancy, Robert Saglio, Brian Hanson, Richard Frank, and Susan Kuse for embracing the concept of home theater and marketing it better than anybody else; Carlos Alvarado and Yadviga Thrun who helped me design the Roxy; my partners, John Thomsen and Eric Seidman, for encouraging me to build it; Chris Esse, Maureen Jenson, Larry Ullman, and Mark Fleischman for 'discovering' me and publishing almost every theater I ever designed in *Audio Video Interiors*; Paige Rense and Michael Wollaeger of *Architectural Digest* who have continued to include my work in their prestigious publication; Keith Yates and Russ Herchelman for choosing to be friends and not rivals; Susan Jonas and Marilyn Nessenson for helping me to realize the concept of this book; Rosemary Pefhany of Irwin Seating, David Leiner of SCS Carpets, David Mason of Krell Lighting, Susan Branch of Scalamandré, and Barry Cohen and David Walczak of F. Schumacher & Co. for their tireless advice and help; Eli Harrary of Harmon International and Giovanni Cozzi of Vidikron for inviting me to join them at CES; and Scott Bronson, Pat Henny, Andrew Oderdonck, Jon Jonasson, Jerry Magusen, Barbara Golden, Frank Pollaro, Pat Motilinsky, Richard Whobery, Carolyn Starter, Jim Belmont, Robert Weingand, Leo Tousley, Ciro De Grezia, Dino Georgiou, Lou Valentino, J.P. Searles, Jay Gibson, Don Lotten, and Henry Rosenblit for all of their help. I am also deeply grateful to all my clients, who believed in me and let me flesh out their dreams; to Bill Curtis for making this book possible; to Brett Anderson, Ken deBie, Michele Locatelli, Sheila Trevett, Robert Ross, and the CurtCo team for blending masterfully words and pictures; and last but not least, to my talented photographer, Phillip Ennis, whose art made my work look better than I had a right to expect.

Theo Kalomirakis

CONTENTS

A Day in Hollywood, a Night in the Ukraine 8
An Introduction by Theo Kalomirakis

When the Movies Come to You 10
An Introduction by Roger Ebert

The Architecture of Imagination 12

The Age of the Movie Palace 20

A Uniquely Social Place 28

The Theaters:

The Ziegfeld 38

The Paramount 54

The Uptown 68

The Apollo 82

The Copper Beach 88

The Gold Coast 98

The Bubble Hill 112

The Cinema 122

The Savoy 132

The Mayfair 138

The Loews Pitkin 152

Credits 164

A Day in Hollywood,

A NIGHT IN THE UKRAINE

If someone had told me only a few years ago that I would one day find myself designing private theaters for individuals around the world, I would have laughed at the absurdity of the idea. Why would I want to abandon a comfortable career as a magazine art director for something that sounded so ridiculously far-fetched and unrealistic?

I discovered the answer to this question in the course of nine breathlessly fast years, during which I found myself—by an unforeseen coincidence of events—designing a theater (the Roxy) in the basement of my house in Park Slope, Brooklyn, appearing as a result on the front page of the *New York Times* and *USA Today*, exciting unsuspecting strangers about the prospect of building their own private theaters, and finally quitting my job to pursue a career in a field in which I had no formal training....

Well, almost none. Movies, after all, were my passion growing up; playing "theater" was another. I remember the movie parties my younger brother and I threw on the rooftop terrace of our house in Athens, Greece. It didn't matter what was on the evening program. Our guests never had enough of our insipid travelogues of journeys down the Nile or up the Amazon (reels borrowed from the American Library in Athens) or hand-tinted, preciously self-conscious excursions into the realm of the avante garde directed by their host—yours truly. All that mattered was that we were gathered under the moonlit Athenian night, enjoying moving pictures, like kids who prefer the magic of their tree houses to the comfort of their actual homes. And nine years after completing the construction of the Roxy in my basement, I still feel like a kid when I go down there to watch a movie with my friends. Submerged in this underground haven, I abandon myself to the

pleasures of celluloid—pleasures I share with guests who come over to take in the thrills of the latest action adventure or the melodrama of the earliest silent epic.

These movies are in themselves a kind of trip—and so has my life been designing theaters. If I were to name only one fringe benefit of my work, I would say without hesitation that it's the travel. We love movies, in part, because they take us to places we've never been before; my job I love for the same reason. I enjoyed working on the Uptown theater not just for the theater itself—the careful assemblage of moldings and lights—but for all the many cross-country flights over the Nevada desert and snow-capped western mountains to

Los Angeles, where I supervised the theater's construction. There have been times when I found myself, all in the same week, driving cautiously along the shores of the Gulf of Mexico past signs warning of alligators crossing the road, sipping coffee at sunrise on Seattle's harbor, or enjoying stimulating conversation over fresh fish and excellent wine under the seaside moonlight of Côte d'Antibes in the south of France.

Of course, I often complain about the debilitating effects of constant travel, but the truth of the matter is that I love the adventure of it. Just recently, I flew for one day from New York to Los Angeles to meet a new client in the Hollywood Hills. The following day, I was back in New York packing for the Ukraine, where I stayed for only one night. There, I met my client, examined the property, took measurements, reflected on the theater to be, then explored the chill night streets of Kiev and got miserably intoxicated on

Russian vodka, all the while thanking God one more time for making whatever talent I have my magic carpet, my box-office ticket to the world.

Each of the theaters presented in this book represents a journey of its own, both geographical and creative. Each has its own history and personality, and each is the tangible result of an intangible process of discovery—for myself as well as for the owner. We have gathered in these pages some of all three—history, personality, and discovery—along with, we hope, a touch of that elusive magic that gives the movies a special place in our imaginations.

THEO KALOMIRAKIS
Brooklyn, New York

WHEN THE MOVIES COME TO YOU
A NEW ERA IN THE HISTORY OF MOVIE-GOING

Henry Ford wanted to put a Model T in every garage. Theo Kalomirakis wants to put a movie theater in every home. Not just a "screening room," but a real theater, re-creating the pizzazz and showmanship of the classic movie palaces of the 1920s, when the lobby was part of the show. My wife, Chaz, and I have one of Theo's dream palaces in our home. Its neon sign announces its name (the Lyric, recalling our first date at Chicago's Lyric Opera). It seats fourteen. The little ticket booth is permanently manned by a life-size mannequin of Oliver Hardy, which began life as a tailor's dummy in Brazil. Next to the Palais Croisette at the Cannes Film Festival, it is my favorite place to watch a movie.

The first giant-screen television I can remember seeing was in Charlie Chaplin's *Modern Times*, where the assembly lines were overseen by a Big-Brother type. The notion that such technology might find its way into the home was suggested in Francois Truffaut's *Farenheit 451* (1967), in which one wall of the living room was given over to a flat-panel TV display. At the time, it seemed like a vision of the future. By 1989, I had one myself.

I love movies, but I hate watching them on small-screen television sets. The experience of the film is diminished; the ambiance is lacking. A movie should be bigger than its audience; it should loom over us; its sound should surround us, and we should be contained by the experience. Robert Mitchum once asked his wife, Dorothy, why she thought movie fans made such a big deal over him. "Bob," she said, "it's because when you're up there on that big screen, they're smaller than your nostril."

When the first rear-projection TV sets came onto the market, I didn't much like them. You had to position yourself just so in front of the screen, and even then the picture lacked focus and clarity. But later models were much improved, and eventually I bought a 45-inch Mitsubishi, and enjoyed it enormously. Of course, I played laserdiscs on it; tapes didn't supply the necessary detail. It was fine. But it was still a television.

In 1988, I was asked to do a frame-by-frame analysis of *Citizen Kane* for a group of students at the Canadian Center for Motion Picture Study outside Toronto. The center, dream-child of director Norman Jewison, had a screening room, including a front-mounted, three-lens TV projector aimed at a large screen. The moment I saw *Kane* on it, I was lost: I had to have one for myself.

Private screening rooms ideally bring the movie experience into the home without greatly diminishing it. At first, they were the playthings of the rich. (I once asked the young son of a studio owner if he went to the movies with his father, and he replied, "Dad says he doesn't go to the movies. The movies come to him.") There is a wonderful book named *The Hollywood Style*, by Arthur Knight, with photographs by Eliot Eliofson, that documents the private screening rooms of Hollywood stars and moguls from the 1920s through the 1960s.

The advent of high-quality projection television and surround sound has brought this plaything of the moguls into the realm of more ordinary people. To be sure, a high-quality home setup isn't cheap. Your own theater, with let's say a 10-foot screen and good sound and a ceiling-mounted projector, can cost from $5,000 (rock bottom, with a one-gun projector) to $12,000 (very

nice) to $25,000 and up (videophile's fantasy). Part of the extra cost will be for a line doubler (or even quadrupler), which is essential for a picture that looks more like a movie and less like a television.

That's assuming you install the equipment in an ordinary room. There is no place for ordinary rooms in the vision of Theo Kalomirakis. A former art director with a love for the great movie palaces of the past, he re-creates on a smaller scale the glorious excesses of the Golden Age of cinema architecture. He sizes up your available space, discusses your memories, assesses the twinkle in your eye, and returns with plans for your own Ziegfeld or Paramount or Mayfair.

Looking through the pages of this book, which represents a cross-section of Theo's work, I am reminded of some of the feelings I had when I first went to the movies. There was a different level of reality inside a movie theater, even

inside the relatively humble palaces of my home town of Urbana-Campaign, Illinois, where the Rialto, the Orpheum, and the Virginia all recalled the glory days of vaudeville and silent films. The architecture helped prepare your mindset for the movie experience. It suggested that reality ended at the door, that dreams were manufactured inside. Every house should have a room like that.

ROGER EBERT

CHICAGO, ILLINOIS

THE ARCHITECTURE OF IMAGINATION

Alexander Dumas the Elder once noted that to create a drama, all one needs is four walls and one passion. Yet the first part of this formula seems, today, largely to have fallen by the wayside. Too frequently, these walls have become synonymous with the box dimensions of a television set haphazardly situated in the home, or—at best—comprise the barren wastes of the local cineplex (the interiors of which remind one of the inside of a refrigerator, whose lights go off when the door is shut). Architecture has always been an integral part of the true theatrical performance. Even a bad movie viewed in a fine theater becomes an entertaining event, whereas that same movie viewed on television or a VCR is simply a bad

film. In a space conceived on a scale equal to and in harmony with the music of imagination, the pitch of emotions amplifies and resounds within its walls.

The architecture of theater is an architecture of escape, for it offers an environment in which the senses and imagination are indulged. It makes possible the suspension of disbelief that allows the drama to assume the full dimensions of life, and so becomes an essential component of the performance. In classical Greece, the theater in fact began as a model of the universe in which the plays of early dramatists, such as Aeschylus, could be enacted. The earth was represented by the circular stage, with heaven, the dwelling place of the gods, depicted by the gallery above, and the underworld below. Originally, Greek dramas employed a single actor, who moved about on an open stage while the chorus to one side commented on his actions, enabling the story to progress. As the members of the chorus

decreased with time (originally there were as many as fifty, later as few as twelve), characters were added to the plot, requiring actors to play double roles; thus, a scenic façade, complete with multiple entrances and exits, was erected toward the back of the stage.

The sophisticated theater design of the Greeks informed the style and dynamics of European theaters for centuries to come. Yet the development of theaters differed according to the type of performance, as well as with the social standards of the region. In England, for example, where the subject matter of

During the Hellenistic Age, more sophisticated architectural techniques, like vaulted structural supports, allowed larger and more lavish theaters, such as this fine example in Segesta, Sicily.

dramas was severely restricted by the establishment of a Protestant national church, concern for adherence to classical rules was almost nonexistent, and playwrights, such as Ben Jonson and William Shakespeare, wrote largely unbound by convention. Settings were conveyed to the audience by the gestures and words of the actors, rather than by elaborate scenery and costumes. Great sixteenth-century British theaters, such as the Swan and the Globe, bore more than a passing resemblance to the earliest Greek theaters, with their permanent rear façades, plain stages, and open-air designs. These theaters were public places with covered galleries and benches (for those who could afford them) and courtyards for standing room on three sides of the raised platform stage.

By contrast, on the Continent, the theaters of the Renaissance consisted mostly of private auditoriums built for the entertainment of a privileged elite and were very much preoccupied with the classical sensibility. These theaters, especially in Italy, relied heavily on visual effects to delight their audiences—fabulous architectural detail, elaborate machinery, and magnificent stage scenery that gained much from the Renaissance

painters' discovery of the principle of perspective. It was in Italy during this period that the first indoor theater was created, the Teatro Olimpico, in Vicenza, allowing stage lighting to assume its place as an important theatrical element.

These ornate Italian theaters, with their tiered circular seating and embellished prosceniums, in their turn, influenced the design of private court theaters throughout Europe for more than one hundred years. During this period, the orchestra pit was added, and the stage area was extended backward to accommodate the increasingly elaborate changes of scenery. The seating arrangements, too, were specialized, reflecting architecturally the social strata so near and dear to noble patrons.

Such court theaters were the original venues of performances for music and operas by artists like Monteverdi and Mozart. Gradually, however, these

Typical of an Elizabethan public playhouse, the Swan (above) comprised an open-air circular courtyard that contained several galleries and standing room on three sides of the stage. No scenery was used, so that scene and location changes had to be conveyed through the dialogue and gestures of the actors. The baroque opulence of theaters like the Paris Opera House (right) reflects the opera's traditional flaunting of patrons' wealth and influence in the form of elaborate staging and costumes.

Court theaters, such as the one built for Louis XV at Versailles
(preceding pages), often served as architectural metaphors for the hierarchy of nobles,
with the highest-ranked audience members occupying the upper balconies and the less-exalted
gentry crowding the orchestra. Old World theaters have found their way into the New as well.
The Asolo Theater (above) was built in the rococo style in 1798; in 1950, it was purchased and
reassembled in its entirety on the grounds of Ca' d' Zan, in Sarasota, Florida,
the residence of showman John Ringling.

aristocratic theaters gave rise to the public opera houses, which were for the most part extensions of the court theaters, varying only in the number of people they could hold. Indeed, the privileged timbre of such palatial halls as the Paris Opera House or Milan's La Scala was inherited directly from the private court theaters, unsullied by the coarseness of the common people. As the centuries progressed, private theaters continued to be built for aristocrats and wealthy individuals (such as John Ringling's Asolo Theater in Sarasota, Florida), as did so-called "high-brow" public theaters, like Covent Garden in London, and the Metropolitan Opera in New York. These venerable institutions pursued and expanded upon the architectural and social traditions that had continued to evolve since the sixteenth century, broadening their audiences to encompass the haute bourgeoisie of the nineteenth century, which became their mainstay. It was not until the early twentieth century that the stylistic grandeur of the old opera houses

and theaters at last mingled with the down-to-earth, somewhat vulgar air of the vaudeville music halls—a feat that owes everything to the technological innovation of the motion picture. For it was the motion picture that brought the working classes and the upper classes together to be entertained; and to house these democratic audiences, as well as to showcase this exciting new art form, a new architectural idiom came into being—one that combined the familiar with the radically new.

The profound impact on audiences of movie palaces, as these theaters came to be called, stands as testimony to the vitality of the dramatic and architechtural traditions from which they evolved. The relationship between design and drama is a symbiotic one:

Mrs. Lyndon Johnson, in 1965, commissioned a private theater in the East Room of the White House. Used for official functions and entertaining, the stage was designed to blend with the executive mansion's historical elements and is portable, though it appears a part of the room.

architectural advances in theater design often prompted dramatic innovation, while new, bolder dramas demanded greater flexibility from the spaces in which they were presented. And nowhere have more demands been made than in the early movie theaters of this century, which stimulated a blend of tradition and innovation in order to accommodate the burgeoning medium of film, yielding some of the most unique and elaborate spaces ever constructed for the purpose of bringing the imagination alive. When M. Dumas prescribed four walls as a necessary component of drama, perhaps he himself had no idea how dramatic those four walls might become, nor how rich a range of passions they might inspire. ◆

Film stars, producers, and directors pioneered the concept of incorporating a moving-picture theater into the home. Here, filmmaker Cecil B. DeMille poses beside his theater's screen, on which is projected a scene from his film *The Plainsman*.

THE AGE OF THE MOVIE PALACE

Theater's Gilded Age began—technically—in 1896, when Thomas Edison (prefiguring the Hollywood taste for exhibitionism) first used his Vitaphone to project the moving image of a dancing nymph onto a large screen at Koster & Bials' Music Hall on Herald Square in New York. In *spirit*, however, it began with the first true movie palaces, the great *grandes dames* of cinema, some of which were hastily converted vaudeville music halls (such as Loew's Herald Square Theatre), others lavishly erected structures consecrated to the worship of the most exciting new medium to emerge since the invention of the printing press—theaters like the Regent, the Capitol, the Strand.

Although by 1905 the motion picture existed as a curiosity, a novelty beneath the well-advertised arches of nickelodeons that appeared across the country, its viability as a permanent and versatile form of entertainment wasn't realized until almost a decade later. It was during the brief span between World War I and the Great Depression that the motion picture came into its own; and it was able to do so only once suitable theaters were built to house its audiences. These theaters drew upon the conventions of so-called "legitimate" theaters for their designs, combining with these silver movie screens and programs whose medleys of singers and dancers owed much to vaudeville. For the price of a sandwich and beer, these enchanted castles could transport you—set you beneath the temples of ancient Egypt or in a lotus-scented garden from *The Arabian Nights*; they could elicit from all who entered an intensity of feeling—the throbbing bass of pathos, the fluttering soprano flight of rapture. Something lived in them: it was as much in the folds of their draperies, in the shadows of their fantastic moldings, as on their screens that the creations of art resided, waiting to be called forth in the beam of a spotlight or the flicker of a projector's reels.

Their creators—architects and visionaries—were surprisingly few, due to the fact that most of the theaters were part of large chains—such as Paramount, Loew or Fox—and the chains' owners tended to favor the talents of a handful of architects who specialized in this field. Thomas W. Lamb, John Eberson,

Grauman's Chinese Theater (opposite), built in 1927, served as Hollywood's high temple. Site of every major film premiere, its searchlights illuminate the Los Angeles night during the 1943 Academy Awards presentation ceremony. The Capitol Theater in Chicago (above) was created in 1923 by John Eberson, whose "atmospheric theaters" were among the most innovative of the great movie palaces.

and Rapp & Rapp have assumed their places in the lore of early cinema as the architects of popular dream.

Lamb, who designed the Regent in New York (the first "deluxe" movie house constructed solely for viewing motion pictures), specialized in theaters that were known for their staid luxury and the excellent views throughout their massive auditoriums. Eberson, on the other hand, was the father of the "atmospheric" theater, in which the auditorium was made to appear like an outdoor amphitheater beneath a starlit sky; he re-created Chinese gardens, Spanish Baroque patios, and Persian mosques in theater auditoriums across the country. The Rapp brothers of Chicago—architects of the famed Paramount on Times Square—were best known for the sheer opulence of their buildings, which ranged in style from Versailles-like grandeur to Art Moderne.

Architecture, however, was but a part of the success formula of these remarkable edifices. For the vision of the early movie-house entrepreneurs played perhaps the most crucial role in fomenting the mystique of the movies. Their personalities shaped the lines of their theaters as much as the architects' drafting pens—just as their names lit up the marquees. And no single individual

Another Los Angeles landmark,
the Pantages (preceding pages) was designed
by architect B. Marcus Priteca in 1930.
It features a lavish arrangement of geometric
patterns radiating from the frosted-glass
chandelier that hangs at the center
of the auditorium. In addition to live
stage shows and movie premieres, during
the 1950s, the Pantages—like Grauman's
Chinese the decade before—hosted
numerous Academy Awards presentations.
Hailed at its opening in 1927
as "the Motion Picture Cathedral,"
S.L. Rothafel's Roxy holds a place of its own
in the movie-palace peerage. Located
a few blocks from Times Square, the Roxy
was equipped with more than 6,000 seats.
Its lobby (above) contained "the world's
largest oval rug," which covered the marble
floor, and a 20-foot crystal chandelier
that hung from the domed ceiling.
Another extraordinary lobby (right) graced
Chicago's Capitol, whose continental flare
drew upon the vocabulary of Europe's
great opera houses.

exerted a greater influence over the art and artifice of theater design than Samuel L. Rothafel, known universally to that generation as "Roxy."

Roxy's career began, in 1908, in the back hall of a tavern in rural Pennsylvania, where he showed his first film, which was projected onto a bedsheet. A resourceful, inventive man with a passion for pictures, Roxy occupied himself constantly in the quest to improve the motion-picture experience: he made curtains that opened to reveal the screen before the show started, concocted a system of lights that saturated the screen, at the flip of a switch, with colors to suit the mood of the scene, and hired live entertainment—singers and musicians—to entertain his audiences between pictures. After hosting a successful radio show in 1925, he opened his own theater in New York, one without peer in movie house history: "the Motion Picture Cathedral." This monument to glamorous excess was named, aptly enough, the Roxy.

Designed by Walter Ahlschlager and built on Seventh Avenue at a cost of $12 million, the Roxy set an entirely new standard for motion-picture theaters—as well as for the science of engineering. With seating for more than 6,200 people and an army of staff,

the Roxy opened on March 11, 1927, to unprecedented fanfare: thousands of spectators crowded the avenue, klieg lights scanned the skies, and hundreds of Manhattan luminaries and stars—including Harold Lloyd, Charlie Chaplin, Norma Talmadge, and Gloria Swanson (whose film *The Love of Sunya* was the main feature)—were in attendance. It was a triumph—and, ironically, the beginning of the end for movie palaces at large.

The Great Depression that followed a few years later made entertainment on the Roxy's scale a losing proposition, and smaller, more manageable theaters took the places of these great halls. Today, only a few of the old movie palaces, with their upholstered velvet and sweeping marble staircases, can still be found. Numerous preservation-minded citizens have worked diligently to save and restore them, and their efforts ought to receive a standing ovation. Yet preservation means more than a new coat of paint or a plaster patch: it requires continuity, an extension of the past into the present, adapting past traditions to present needs.

In a sense, this revitalization of tradition is what the work of designer Theo Kalomirakis is all about. A student and devotee of film, he has made a career for himself by bringing together two important elements: the brilliant high

style of the movie palace and the amenity of the private theater. He has also brought to his work the charisma, imagination, and passion for film of a latter-day Roxy, laboring to make the most of the movie experience. Like the great movie-palace architects, drawing upon and reinterpreting a panoply of architectural traditions, Kalomirakis creates an environment flavored with a sense of history, nostalgia, and romance. His designs are neither historic nor quite modern: like the old movie houses on which they are based, they are places out of time—worlds unto themselves wherein almost anything becomes possible. ➤

The Ohio Theatre (left) was designed by Thomas W. Lamb and opened in Columbus in 1928, dazzling moviegoers with its Mexican Baroque ornamentation. Atlanta's Fox (above), built in 1929, boasted the largest curved Cinemascope screen in the world. An atmospheric theater, the auditorium resembled a Moorish city, complete with minarets and castellated walls.

A Uniquely Social Place

One of the numerous odd paradoxes of American life is that the most indisputably American among us are often those most recently arrived. We tend, as a nation, to identify with immigrants (all of us being, at some level and at some time, transplants ourselves); but more than this, we embrace as Americans certain qualities of originality and adaptability that immigrants embody. Our daily lives are a patchwork of clippings from other cultures—the hot dog, St. Patrick's Day, Christmas trees. The same can be said of the movie palace. Certainly it is no coincidence that both Thomas W. Lamb and John Eberson, two of the greatest American theatrical architects, were immigrants—the former from Scotland, the latter from Austria. Each of these men—and others like them—brought to the rather soberly serious, practical, and well-regimented American architectural landscape of the early century a breath of romance—a mist from Arcadia, a lotus-scented breeze. And the strange extravagance of their designs, their exotic ventures, permanently shaped our common notion of what a movie theater should be, while at the same time contributing to the establishment of a standard of taste that would characterize this brief period in our history as one of innovation and excess.

Just as these men brought to their time and place a fresh perspective onto the architectural scene, so Theo Kalomirakis—whose designs fill this volume—brings to our concept of the movie palace tradition a fresh idiom of line and color quite his own. Having grown up under the influence of films and great architecture, he might seem to have been predestined for his present career as a designer of private movie theaters; but, in fact, his career was largely accidental. Raised in Athens, under the shadow of the Acropolis (a structure whose charms, he sheepishly admits, were lost on him as a child:

The Royal, designed for a Canadian businessman, boasts a grand foyer (opposite) whose walls are covered with mahogany paneling. Solid brass sconces and door frames complement the brass-coffered ceiling. A pair of temple dogs flanks the steps. Mahogany doors (above) lead from the Royal's marquee entrance into the intimate foyer. The outer floor is black granite with diamond-shaped inlays and reflects the marquee sign's incandescent bulbs.

The Royal's auditorium makes use of overlapping wall panels
upholstered with Scalamandré tapestry fabric to enhance the overall acoustics.
Italian Renaissance Ionic columns punctuate the procession of seats that
descends toward the proscenium. The coved ceiling bears a fresco mural inpsired
by Renaissance designs. The mahogany chairs, covered in F. Schumacher's
Gainsborough velvet, are Quinette—the same style used at the
auditorium of the Opera of Paris.

he wondered why the authorities didn't bulldoze it to gain a better view of the sea), Kalomirakis spent as much time as he could enfolded in the dark of the cinema or reading about American films in magazines. He has, to this day, his scrapbook from those early years, an album pasted full of yellowed clippings, whose ragged optimism, from page to page, suggests the ambitions already forming in the young man's mind. "It is true what they say about Americans—or American culture—colonizing the subconscious," Kalomirakis reflects. "That's what happened to me. I grew up with these images of popular culture, and my fantasy was always to come to the United States. Of course, the United States as I experienced it through magazines was not realistic—but I had this strong sense of a new world with its own great music, its own great movies, its own great writing. So when I finally managed to get here, you can imagine my satisfaction—when the fantasy did not exist anymore, but became instead a reality."

This metamorphosis occurred when Kalomirakis was admitted to the film program at New York University, where he could at last indulge the longing to immerse himself in movies and all other things American. "I was so happy not to have to deal with the fantasy," he recalls, "that I would sometimes wake up in the middle of the night, sweating from a nightmare that I was back in Greece with my legs cut off, so that I couldn't walk back to the States. I would touch my legs and say, 'Thank God, I'm still in my apartment on First Avenue.'"

Having realized this particular dream—of living in New York—however, there remained many more still to conquer. After completing his graduate studies (during which he supported himself by odd jobs) and producing his thesis film (which was shown at the New York Film Festival), Kalomirakis switched professions, from film to newspaper. He discovered he had a keen eye

The Roxy, Kalomirakis' first theater—the one that started it all. The arches that line the corridor—the actual foundations of the brownstone—were used as the theater's main architectural element.

A French Renaissance influence pervades the Loew's Grand in Glastenbury, Connecticut, where ornate decorative plasterwork is gilded and glazed over with patina. Corridors on the left and right lead to the powder rooms on one side and the marquee entrance on the other.

for graphic design—a skill that led to design positions at Time, Inc. and Forbes. His interest in cinema took the form of a weekend hobby: he acquired a Hi Fi VCR and began collecting tapes; later, he bought a laserdisc player and, in his own words, became a "movie impresario." He held all-day "movie orgies," screening films for friends and co-workers in the basement of his townhouse, which he converted to a dedicated viewing room complete with genuine theater seats.

As the complexity of the project progressed, yet another twist would be added to an already serpentine career. Articles on his theater, accompanied by

photographs of him "munching popcorn," appeared in the *New York Times* and *USA Today*, fueling his interest in the impact of environment on the movie experience. After moving into a sizeable townhouse in Parkslope in Brooklyn, New York, he created more than just a dedicated viewing room: the basement of his new home emerged as the Roxy, his first true theater, awash in velvet curtains and red-and-blue neon. The result, once word got out, was both unpredictable and immediate: first came occupying armies of magazine photographers, then television crews, including *Entertainment Tonight*. "They did a five-minute story," recalls Kalomirakis.

"When you get one bit of national exposure, fifteen others follow." Soon, his phone rang off the hook. Estée Lauder's son called, inquiring whether Kalomirakis could design a theater for him. Another phone call preceded a cavalcade of limousines from which an entourage of be-suited Japanese businessmen issued, bowing as they filed down the narrow stairs like Biblical kings come to pay homage to Kalomirakis' brainchild. Yet, while this whirlwind of attention spun round him, Kalomirakis remained happily employed as an art director for Forbes, indifferent to the opportunity at hand. In fact it was a member of the Forbes family who finally urged him to regard theater design as a new career. At that point, after some thought, says Kalomirakis, "I decided to break."

Like S.L. Rothafel's decision to open his Family Theatre in Forest City, Pennsylvania, in 1908, Kalomirakis' choice marked the beginning of a creative journey that would crisscross the continent, drawing upon rich architectural traditions, as well as that very American sense of showmanship. Kalomirakis also has in common with the original inventors of the movie palace a deep understanding of the power of fantasy and the role environment plays in the enjoyment of films. "My older clients," he explains, "fantasize about experiencing the movies the way they did when they were kids. They dressed up and took a bus or a train downtown to a movie palace, where they were transported to a world that real life could never get close to."

Kalomirakis' intimate knowledge of that world of the theater, its present and past, informs his own particular brand of social art. "My drawings," he notes, "are the framework for what is really a social kind of architecture. Theaters are uniquely social places, where all of us are watching the same images—watching them differently, perhaps, but always together, there in the dark." ❧

The Bijou in San Marino, California, uses authentic Art Déco elements throughout. The fabric on the walls incorporates a Frank Lloyd Wright design and is manufactured by F. Schumacher. In lieu of curtains, the Bijou's screen is concealed by panels decorated with a pattern copied in various exotic wood veneers and bronze inlays from the elevator doors of New York's famous Chrysler building.

The Theaters

The house, encompassing some 30,000 square feet of irregular rooms, appears to have simply happened—which is to say, it has a self-contained logic of its own. A strange harmony presides: lions and lambs—or more exactly, Déco, Regency, and Frederick Remington—all lie down peaceably together. This eclectic spirit suspends one's disbelief, holds one in a delightful half-dream wherein paradoxes seem perfectly natural. And paradoxes abound: "The house, when we bought it, was just an old-fashioned contemporary," explains Mrs. Barry Knispel, chatelaine of this architectural curiosity. "I don't even know why we wanted to buy it. The back was all straight, just some windows, very ugly. It doesn't even look like the same place. Anyone would see in two minutes what we did."

But one can see very little in two minutes of a house that took five years to build, and which—in its eccentricities, contradictions, and generous humor—symbolizes the hearts and

minds of its owners. Mr. Knispel is a businessman, owner of a major tool manufacturer, whose handshake conveys a sincerity and warmth that is often lacking (or perhaps just worn out) in men of his experience. Mrs. Knispel, who is recovering from agoraphobia, sparkles demurely like pale crystal; still, though she is reclusive, her personality dominates the house. Mr. Knispel has his study and his own media room (there are three on the second floor), but for him, his office and business associates make up the majority of his daily world. The limits of Mrs. Knispel's world, on the other hand, stopped for years at the front doors. When she speaks of "the outside," she does so with a mixture of trepidation and longing: one senses that the house represents, on some level, an attempt to bring "the outside" in. Though the Ziegfeld was predominantly her husband's passion, the theater is the culmination of this ideal—an escape. "When I start walking down that staircase on a Saturday night," she

Original three-sheet posters (preceding pages) fill the 40-foot lobby's display cases, which are framed by ebonized mahogany pilasters and bird's-eye maple wainscoting with ebony inlay. The carpet (above left) is a Schumacher reproduction of Donald Deskey's "musical instruments" design for Radio City Music Hall. The lacquered bird's-eye maple, stainless-steel, and ebony doors (above right) are reproductions of the elevator doors of the Bullock's Wilshire in Los Angeles.

admits, "I just walk into another atmosphere. I can't really explain it; it's just weird."

The staircase winds around a circular elevator shaft, leading to a well-insulated lower level. Here, the hallway uncurls suddenly in a half circle, lit brilliantly by marquee lights and pulsing red and yellow neon bars reflected in a floor of polished black granite. One finds oneself on an inlaid sidewalk before the burled doors of the Ziegfeld Theater, circa 1930, in whose Déco booth the droopy-eyed ticket-seller yawns, head in hands. Stainless-steel sconces illuminate vintage posters bearing the concupiscent curves of box-office blond Betty Grable and June Allyson. Through doors copied from the Bullock's Wilshire in Los Angeles lies the concession room—a gleaming black and crimson lounge, spliced here and there with a slice of steel—where one can pause to sip a soda beneath the glimmer of a Lalique chandelier. To the left of the ticket booth, behind an identical set of doors, is the theater proper, moodily lit by Déco lanterns and recessed lights, which cast shadows across the ornate coffered ceiling. Fifteen plush silk-upholstered seats are arranged before the red velvet curtains that, when they part, reveal a galaxy of fiber-optic stars.

"It's like you just get lost in time," exclaims Mrs. Knispel. "You come down here after a hard day's work, and it's movie time. It's not an every-night television theater, like the ones upstairs. We get our popcorn and our sodas when we come down here, and we go out."

The Ziegfeld, she explains, in a small way, brings the world to her: friends, her nephew, even occasionally her husband's business associates. "This is great," she says. "You can have a special movie for company. On the Fourth of July, when we had a big party, we had so many people who wanted to see movies that we had to have two showings—one at one o'clock and another at four, before the barbecue."

Constructing this home, however, meant bringing a great deal more of the world to the doorstep than perhaps at first

Light flares through the frosted crystal geometry of the foyer's chandelier, created by René Lalique in France, circa 1928. The red leather armchairs and sofa in the foyer are by Dakota Jackson. The foyer also features a fully equipped bar complete with an ice-cream fountain and popcorn machine.

Mrs. Knispel was prepared to greet. Armies, in fact: designers, contractors, installers—an occupying force, among whose ranks skirmishes would sometimes break out. The house's decorator and the builder, like rival generals, would countermand one another's orders, the builder insisting that the decorator's plans defied physical laws: when the latter wanted a beam removed, the former protested, "But that's a bearing beam." "I don't care," the decorator answered. "You can fix it some other way." "But," he told her, "it's holding up three walls!" "Just get it out," she said.

Peacemaker was not a role into which Mrs. Knispel easily slipped. "I was going out of my mind," she sighs, "so my doctors said, 'Tell your husband that you do not want to hear about the house for six months.' So I told him I couldn't take the stress."

Building the Ziegfeld, however, proved a bright spot amid this dreary confusion. "Theo," Mrs. Knispel says, "is not like other people. He's not selling you, he's telling you about these times, what people did and what

they liked. He just mesmerizes you. He told me, 'I'm giving you a piece of yesterday, and every time you come down here, you're going to be stepping out of your home into the past.' That's what Theo said would happen, and it did. This was the nicest part about building this whole house—the most pleasant and, of course, the most lovely part."

Her sole complaint, in fact, might be that the Ziegfeld is *too* pleasant—that too much of "the outside" has found its way in. Months of concentrated therapy have enabled her to venture out of her private Oz; but when her husband took off a few days from work, and as a surprise, she asked him to choose one movie he'd like to see, "he didn't want to do it. 'I like my theater better,' he said."

And so, she adds, patting their woolly heads, do Andy and Rose, for unlike the local cineplex, the Ziegfeld welcomes them. They sit in the theater chairs to watch; and when their favorite movie, *The Incredible Journey*, plays, they run up to the screen and bark during

The candy counter is incorporated into the bar using custom-designed stainless-steel inlays. The varnished woodgrain and steel patterns found on the cabinets repeat the motif of the theater's Déco-style auditorium and foyer doors.

the more climactic moments. "You'd be surprised," she says. "They love that movie with the dogs and cats."

Thus the Ziegfeld works its magic on humans and canines alike, its elegantly inlaid doors opening, for the house's inhabitants, upon a wider outside world—or offering, at least, a step in that direction. A step into another reality. A step into the past. ◆

The Ziegfeld theater's auditorium, upholstered in black Ultrasuede, has a silver-leaf ceiling and cove, which, like the entire room, is bathed in the glow of fiber-optic lighting that changes hue, offering virtually limitless combinations of color. The silk-covered chairs are custom-designed.

The Paramount

A BEAUX ARTS PALACE BRINGS BACK
THE GRANDEUR OF THE MOVIE HOUSE

———◆———

The Paramount's owner, Mr. Charles Steven Cohen,

is a man who thinks quite naturally in terms of scale.

He himself is not unusually tall, but his high Brooks Brothers

polish (leather braces, cream-smooth shirts, bright harlequin ties)

and slim, sinewy hands, consummately manicured, give him

an elongated appearance, an illusion of greater height.

Add to these traits his salt-and-peppered hair (expertly trimmed)

and obsidian eyes, and one begins to get an idea of the presence

he possesses. He seems to blend a finely tuned aesthetic sensibility

with a studied toughness, making him something of

a cross between John Gilbert and George Raft.

The Paramount's solid brass marquee is electrified by incandescent
lighting, while the pavement features a genuine terrazzo floor. The walls
are limestone with mahogany poster frames designed to represent
a street setting; this open-air effect is enhanced by fiber-optic stars.
Near the entrance (above), a silk-screen reproduction of a typical
period box-office sign stands beside movie-poster display cases.
The turn-of-the-century-style sconces are custom-made
from solid brass. The box-office mannequin (right)
is by Lisa Lichtenfels.

Of course, this is a sloppy comparison, one that would likely draw criticism from Mr. Cohen, who brings to his enthusiasm for film a connoisseur's concern for precision and detail (as a matter of fact, he has written a best-selling book on movie trivia), but one that is nevertheless apropos. For as he himself says, "Movies so enveloped my whole life. When I was three, I saw *Cinderella*. It was my first experience." So it comes as no surprise that this fascination with the big screen should filter into his own larger-than-life personal style.

A modern Maecenas in every respect, Mr. Cohen runs a major Manhattan real estate concern with all of the fervor (and ferment) that entails. There is about him a commotion in keeping with the most blustering studio boss, and his offices, with their vertiginous penthouse vistas of Manhattan, recall the New York idyll envisioned by many a Hollywood set designer. As for his weekend home—a varnished wood-and-stone edifice resembling a Nordic fortress—it suggests a widescreen epic adventure: one half expects sword-wielding Norsemen to ride from the gate or medieval vassals to bow down at the threshold. Instead, one

is greeted by the groundskeeper, a grizzled middle-aged man with a very unadventurous disposition, who grumblingly escorts one down a winding stairwell to Mr. Cohen's theater—an incandescent tribute to its owner's cinematic devotion.

Although the plans for the house called for a theater/screening room of significant size, Mr. Cohen had originally assumed that this would be contemporary in design. When he met Kalomirakis, however, their collaboration led them down other, more nostalgic paths. The theater, which seats twenty-four, was the largest that Kalomirakis had yet attempted and offered some enticing possibilities, due largely to the enormous dedicated space left unfinished during the home's construction. "We were able to provide Theo with a very high ceiling, which allowed him to attain a scale he had been unable to achieve before," notes Mr. Cohen, who was personally involved with every phase of the theater's development. "Through Theo's hard work and research and attention to detail, a wonderful set of plans and specs and finishes was presented for our approval." These plans called for a theater designed in the Beaux Arts style,

The brass handles on the doors are originals from the Paramount Theater
on Times Square. The chandelier, which dates from 1919, was salvaged from the old
Centrum Theater in Cleveland, whose restoration Kalomirakis recently supervised.
The walls feature solid mahogany wainscoting. Bar-seat fabric is by Scalamandré.
Silk-screened period signs (above) found throughout the Paramount are custom-made.
The Marquee entrance (following pages) leads past the box office into the main foyer.
A carved mahogany mantle in the foyer supports an antique
bronze doré clock, circa 1880.

in the tradition of the really grand old movie houses—much to Mr. Cohen's delight: "I was not old enough to be able to experience the types of theaters we replicated. They were just in disrepair or nonexistent. However, my movie-going experience preceded the multiplexes of contemporary design. It was the old RKOs, the Orpheums, the old vaudeville theaters that were converted for film use. These were my memories, and this was a new, clean, exciting replication that I had never had the chance to experience."

This melding of contemporary and past is both figurative and literal: Kalomirakis discovered the ornate ceiling panels at Warner Brothers' Burbank studios, as well as the push bars from the old Paramount's doors, which can be seen on those of the new Paramount. (These push bars, incidentally, were the inspiration for the theater's name.) In addition, the lobby's chandelier was removed and restored from an old Cleveland theater.

If anything, however, it is the two-story auditorium that gives the

theater its authenticity. Backlit filigree panels, gilding, and tapestry-upholstered baffles immerse one in a lush, *autre temps* atmosphere that transports one completely as one descends the tiered rows of seats. "It is another time and place," exclaims Mr. Cohen. "It absolutely convinces you that you are in an old theater. This echoes the vision of the past through today's eyes, gives you the ability to reach back to incorporate many of the elements of old that made film-going a total experience. Something's been lost in the way we see video today. This theater helps to restore the film experience to its original larger-than-life dimensions, which precede the advent of television."

This love of the "true movie-going experience" is something Mr. Cohen intends to pass along to his children, ages seven and eleven. It is his way of imparting to them the imaginative world that formed his own consciousness—in the hope that, in some small way, it will help to form theirs, "rather than the hyperkinetic world of MTV and junk editing. They're experiencing what I experience."

The auditorium's ceiling lanterns (right), from **Urban Archaeology of New York,** are reproductions of a *fin de siècle* design. The medallions from which the lanterns hang are custom-molded. The valances are Scalamandré silk, while the wall panels are covered in a tapestry upholstery, also by Scalamandré. The filigree grilles (above) were cast from a French Renaissance design.

And to tell the truth, Mr. Cohen, on the subject of his theater, is himself not unlike an enraptured youth holding forth at length on the virtues of a favorite bicycle. He will, he announces, change the posters and marquees regularly (his poster collection is extensive, boasting both the celebrated and obscure), and he continually tinkers with the theater's equipment: "I'm upgrading," he confides. "I'm staying state-of-the-art, staying on the cutting edge, because it makes the experience that much more real, more exciting. These are projected images like none I've ever seen."

Whether it's Frank Capra or the Three Stooges, nothing, for Mr. Cohen, can ever take the place of the big screen, which has always served as his wide-angle window on the world. ❧

The auditorium carpet is by Stark, New York. The ceiling panels are from original coffer moldings discovered and then fabricated by the Warner Brothers staff shop. Renaissance-style filigree grilles are cast in bronze and backlit. The ceiling cove is stenciled with gold-leaf accents. Genuine theatrical footlights illuminate the stage. The chairs, by Irwin Seating, are upholstered in Schumacher's Gainsborough velvet.

The Uptown

A TOY FOR CHILDREN OF ALL AGES

◆

It's fitting that the Uptown should be located in

Southern California, a part of the country known for its theme parks,

if no longer for its citrus groves. While the street's other residences

are constructed for the most part in the characteristic California-

ranch idiom—single-story sprawling rooftops and post-strewn

porches—the Uptown's eccentric home is a towering stack

of crenelated gables, turrets, minarets, and Elizabethan latticework.

It's as if, from a magic bean, Toad Hall or Sleeping Beauty's castle

has blossomed in this well-tended garden of suburban serenity.

But then, the house was created, from foundation to rafters,

for the purpose of pure amusement.

Take as an example the front lawn, resplendent with a rainbow of blossoms, on whose velvety expanse Chia people cavort in straw hats (one even climbs the trellis). In the rear garden, the pool nestles in the shade of a man-made grotto of lava rock, peopled with life-size Disney characters from *The Little Mermaid*: lobsters, octopi, crabs, and—curled conspicuously in an oversized oyster shell—Ariel, the little mermaid herself.

In the entry hall, the glass-banistered staircase winds past a two-story mural depicting the Hollywood sign to the floor above, where room after room bristles with electric show lights, toys, works of art, and musical instruments. Glass curio cases glitter with porcelain cartoon characters—Daffy Duck, Bugs Bunny, the Tasmanian Devil, Mickey and Minnie Mouse. Miniature carousels and a Ferris wheel blaze and begin to turn at the press of a switch to the circus-show syncopation of a calliope. Works of art—original lithographs of the Macy's Parade, Rodeo Drive, the Statue of Liberty, and, of course, the Magic

Kingdom—adorn a maze of walls like brilliant jewels scattered across a velvet display case. A statue of a classical ballet dancer in bronze pirouettes beside a wooden moose in a butler's uniform. Beyond a partition hung with a dozen watercolors, another chamber—its walls lined with wainscoting taken from an antique railway car—contains a vintage jukebox and a player piano whose keys rattle out the melody to "When Irish Eyes Are Smiling." Farther along, one discovers the butt-end of a caboose protruding from a wall, its lantern swinging above the door. This is the "Train Room," which consists of untold square footage devoted to a model transcontinental rail-road that takes passengers from Grand Central Station, past the 1939 World's Fair, to the San Francisco Bay.

The effect of this menagerie is a little overwhelming—not unlike the sensory assault one experiences the first time one steps out onto Times Square after dark. Yet, despite the heady surroundings, this castle's keeper, Mr. Larry Kay, is an unassuming

Both incandescent and neon lights flash across the Uptown marquee, which is 17 feet high. The doors (above) are fashioned from a grille that originally belonged to a Boston bank built in 1928. Elements from this same grille appear as wainscoting beneath backlit poster displays. Paddle-wheel lights in the title arch blink in sequence to create the illusion that they're turning.

Gold, bronze, and silver leaf cover the ceiling's tulip-motif panels molded
from those in the Pantages Theater in Los Angeles. The chandelier of stainless
steel and frosted glass is a French original in the Cleopatra style of the early '30s.
Looking into the foyer from the entrance, one finds a fully operable soda fountain.
The foyer's main feature (following pages) is an original lithograph three-sheet
poster of *The Man I Married*, 1940, Twentieth Century Fox.

The theater (named after the cinema in Chicago his wife used to frequent as a young girl) greets visitors at the top of the stairs. Its stainless-steel and frosted-glass doors (taken from a Boston bank) open beneath the twinkling neon marquee upon the foyer, which houses a box office diligently manned by a soft-sculpture ticket-seller in white gloves and pince-nez. The foyer ceiling bears an ornate bronze-, silver-, and gold-leaf panel molded from one belonging to the Pantages Theater in Los Angeles. The chandelier is a French antique, but the 1940s-style stainless-steel soda fountain, though fully equipped with seltzer and chocolate syrup, is a meticulous reproduction, its spigots, levers, and cupboards gleaming remnants of a vanished American institution. "We moved it up from downstairs,"

Mr. Kay points out. "We wanted a soda fountain, and our decorator knew a place that does them. They made it look '40s. They retro-designed it. They did the glass and silverware for us, too."

The auditorium, reached through a pair of portholed mahogany doors, lies beneath the starlit sunset of an Egyptian night. The ceiling cove, lined with a frieze copied from a theater building in Kalomirakis' own Brooklyn neighborhood, shields lights that flare or dim to create a burnished-horizon effect. There are eighteen seats, each of which is accented with side-molding copied from 1930 molds, while the striking Egyptian figures to either side of the proscenium were borrowed from the Pantages Theater's marquee. The mood harkens to the era of the Hollywood spectacle, when epic-scale directors like

Cecil B. DeMille and D.W. Griffith brought the scope of ancient worlds to the screen. It's an era and a style of which Mr. Kay is exceedingly fond: "Today, we've lost the sense of what theaters were all about when I was growing up," he observes from his seat, reclining in the Uptown's lime-lit glow. "Theaters today are just slapped together—they don't make them enjoyable enough to even sit there and look up and say, 'Gosh, we're in a beautiful place.' The Paramounts, the Roxys, the Capitols— they were gorgeous. That's what makes a theater for me—being in a place that's beautiful, old, and picturesque."

The two Egyptian figures are copies of ones that can still be seen above the marquee of the Pantages Theater. The atmospheric ceiling glows with fiber-optic stars. Specialized lights situated behind the cove create sunrise and sunset effects. A Schumacher fabric covers the acoustical panels, the drapery, and the seating. The seats are from Irwin Seating, New York.

The Uptown, in its own way, is all of these things, re-creating in a vivid palette the theatrical haunts of Mr. Kay's Brooklyn youth. Although his own children are grown (the youngest is twenty-nine), Mr. Kay, in the lush half-dark of the Uptown, seems as young as the kid who, in the late 1930s, breathlessly waited for the curtain to rise on his first picture, Disney's *The Reluctant Dragon*. Even though he and his wife frequently go out to the movies, the truer cinematic experience is still found here, where he can view his favorite classics again and again on the big screen. "I would rather see a movie from the '30s, '40s, or '50s than from the '70s, '80s, or '90s," he remarks, "if I have my choice. I like to collect the old ones, and the only way you can see them on the big screen is to create your own big screen. Coming up here and sitting down in these nice seats and picturing yourself in this theater is fun. If you like movies," he laughs, "you've got to like it!" And the kid in Mr. Kay happily does. ⬥

The Apollo

EUROPEAN POLISH IN THE AMERICAN WEST

"I have no patience; I have always taught myself what I wanted to

learn—sailing, auto racing, golf." So says Bernie Thewalt, owner

of the Apollo theater, in a clipped Teutonic accent whose punctilious

abruptness belies the spark of his equally Teutonic blue eyes.

His observable qualities—his proud posture, his angular features,

which flirt with resemblance to certain portraits by Dürer—as he

shakes one's hand, seem to rise up in conflict with his peculiar dress.

Not that, for Southern California in winter, his dress is really

peculiar: chinos, sandals, a brightly tinted Hawaiian-style

shirt. But his ascetic, very European temperament is

as little consonant with his clothing as an eagle

flocked in the tropical feathers of a macaw.

The auditorium furnishes audiences with custom seats imported from Germany. Toward the rear of the theater, the mahogany-and-granite bar houses the Apollo's equipment. The walls are of glazed, rough-textured plaster. The sculptural elements that run the length of the room support the surround speakers and are made of zebrawood paneling arranged in a checkered pattern.

This incongruity carries to his surroundings, as well. His home, a glass and cement crescendo of order, balance, provides the climax to the winding symphonic suite of desert scenery that accompanies visitors to its doorstep. The San Jacinto Mountains loom above the cluster of desert communities that pinwheel outward from the town of Palm Springs, sheltering the sand-swept currents of Paleozoic riverbeds, portions of which have been recently cultivated into lawns, golf courses. On one of these lush fairways, the house perches, a clean, contemporary sculpture displayed upon its rough-hewn pedestal.

In harmony with the immense, stretching landscape beyond their predominantly glass walls, the rooms suggest distance, openness. This comes as no surprise, for, like the landscape, the rooms are formed of air, light, and stone. Various granite forms, polished as if by river water, gleam against the clean, white walls. Streamlined European furnishings—deep-blue leather sofas, black-lacquered chairs and tables—gather to create

small islands afloat in generous spaces, while a Steinway grand piano occupies a space all its own at one end of the living room. "It is from Germany," Mr. Thewalt proudly remarks, then adds, with a note of apology, "The piano is my one effort in teaching myself that failed. I have given up."

Mr. Thewalt clearly takes his amusements seriously. His motive for purchasing a home in the United States (he and his wife, Iris, live six months of the year in the town of Saarbrücken, Germany, and also own an estate in Toulouse, France) is that he could find no one in his native country who plays golf often enough and well enough to keep up with him. His son stationed firmly at the helm of the family's asphalt business, Mr. Thewalt is now free to pursue his interests wherever he pleases. In addition to sailing and golf, he has a keen passion for fine wines. Another passionate pastime is the cinema. And in the Apollo, this passion finds expression.

Located on the house's lower level, the Apollo (named for a

An architectural element known as a "floating ceiling" conceals the recessed projector. The bar counter provides additional bar-style seating.

long-vanished theater in Saarbrücken) draws upon the contemporary idiom of the rest of the house for its flavor. Entering the theater, one descends into the circular foyer, whose round walls are paneled with mahogany and whose floor is made of polished, quartz-flecked black granite. To one side, a door flanked by vintage posters (*Meet Me in Las Vegas, Death Valley Gunfighter*) leads into the auditorium. The seats, imported from Europe, are stylized armchairs into which Mr. Thewalt and his friends can comfortably sink. Checkered zebrawood panels combine with geometric shapes of painted wood (some of them backlit) to relieve the rectangular uniformity of the room, which was originally intended as a gym. Mr. Thewalt decided to convert it to a theater when he grew tired of the area's cineplexes.

"They have no character," he complains, "no soul. And then they are so far away." The Apollo suffers from neither shortcoming. For, after watching a favorite film, Mr. Thewalt and his fellow golfers have only to travel a few steps outdoors to take in another round. ❧

Upholstered panels to either side of the screen soften the emphasis on hard services elsewhere in the room, while absorbing sound reflections to enhance the acoustics.

The
Copper Beach

AN ARTISTIC FIND FOR
A CONTEMPORARY COLLECTOR

———◆———

They say that taste is something you are born with.

(One glance at the conspicuous sartorial landscape of a summer's day

at the beach suffices to demonstrate the truth of this.) But often

the instinct for quality, for style, does not find means of expression

until later in life. Such has been the case with Mr. Weiss,

a sought-after corporate attorney whose political influence extends

to the loftiest echelons of state. One writes "Mr. Weiss" here because

one cannot imagine attaching to this thoughtfully dignified figure a

Christian name—his countenance and bearing demand

reciprocation, a certain distance, a certain respect. His energy

(controlled, thoroughly directed) registers in each gesture—

the opening of his hand, the emphasis on a word—as though he states his case before an unseen bench when he talks of his extensive collection of art: "I came to art sort of late," he explains, "because I wasn't brought up with it. It's a little scary. When you buy something that you understand, it's quite easy. But when you don't entirely understand the object in question, it's a challenge."

Mr. Weiss met that challenge with the same systematic determination that he brings to preparing a client's case for court. He spent several years developing his personal aesthetic sense in order to discover whether his choices held firm. "In the beginning, you see big splashy colors," he says, "and you think, 'That's beautiful.' Then, after a while, when you've looked at it enough, you sometimes get tired of it. You realize it's not as creative as you'd like art to be. That's when you begin to read."

After seven or eight years of reading, Mr. Weiss tentatively began to buy. On business trips, whatever city he happened to be in, if he had an hour or two free, he would visit a couple of galleries, a habit he picked up from a client of the first law firm at which he practiced. This client, he recalls, would leave a board meeting and vanish mysteriously—no one knew where he went, though doubtless speculation abounded. One day, however,

Mr. Weiss discovered that the gentleman's clandestine rendezvous were aesthetic rather than prurient: he made the rounds of art dealers and galleries, amassing a collection of such quality that a major museum was eventually named for him. "I'm not even in his category," Mr. Weiss insists. "But I essentially did the same thing."

Though no museum (as yet) bears his name, Mr. Weiss' home does his treasures equal justice. Tucked like a luminous pearl within the rustic outer shell of Long Island's Oyster Bay, the house is an harmonious *ménage* of angles and curves in a variety of materials, from concrete and slate to tree bark (which, sliced paper-thin, covers the walls of the guest bathroom), providing varied backdrops for the numerous works by Picasso, Warhol, and Cristo (among others) that dwell there. Mr. Weiss had the structure designed to his exacting specifications for the purpose of displaying these remarkable pieces. At the same time, however, he wanted his home to blend with its surroundings of woods, lawns, shimmering bay, and historic architecture. "One of the things that I tried to achieve," he relates, "is a sensitivity to tradition. When I sit here and look out the window, I see a very traditional setting. You have Teddy Roosevelt's Sagamore Hill down the road, and you're looking across the

The sign above the Copper Beach's marquee entrance
(preceding pages) is composed of softly backlit three-dimensional letters
of brushed steel—a style typical of the 1930s. The sconces in the foyer are 1930s
Art Déco antiques, as is the pewter-and-glass chandelier.
The original Warhol silk-screen is of Garbo in *Mata Hari*.

Behind the last row, a mezzanine area was created for a sofa, which offers more informal seating. Ceiling spotlights cast their glow on studio portraits of Humphrey Bogart, Greta Garbo, and Errol Flynn. The arches enhance the perspective looking toward the screen and emphasize the proscenium as the room's focal point.

bay at Center Island, where there are a lot of stately old homes. I'm sticking this contemporary house in the middle of it, so I wanted the transition to be gradual. When you drive onto the property, the placement of the house, the driveway, provides that transition. It's not linear. And the theater within the home is that way also."

The home bears toward the landscape the same relationship as the theater does to the remainder of the house. Located on a lower level, the Copper Beach (named for the property on which the house stands) incorporates elements of the home while retaining its own distinct identity. The marquee entrance consists of a backlit sign above relatively unembellished glass and doors that open onto the foyer. Here, gray paneled walls with a horizontal piping furnish the setting for Mr. Weiss' original silk-screen portrait of Greta Garbo by Andy Warhol. Encircling this prized picture are a frosted-glass chandelier and sconces, as well as a console fashioned from a radiator grille—all of them antique French Art Déco objects, circa 1930. The auditorium—though it measures only twenty-six feet by eighteen feet—creates an effect of spaciousness, thanks to the concentric backlit arches

that lead from the entrance down toward the stage's proscenium. Horizontal bands, accentuated by the lighting scheme, lend an illusion of greater length to the room.

The careful configuration of the rooms is consistent with the design of the rest of the house, for Mr. Weiss neither likes rooms to be overly large nor overly small. "When a space gets too big," he observes, "it loses its identity. On the other hand, I hate being encapsulated, which was one concern I had about the theater. I don't like space enclosed with no windows. I don't feel that way in the theater, however, because its movement travels outward as well. I don't feel confined."

This sense of openness, combined with a very contemporary styling, strikes the perfect note for the Copper Beach's owner, whose philosophy—both aesthetic and personal—is decidedly forward-looking. "My personality is such that I hate to look back," he admits. "I'm not a nostalgic person. My wife likes to go back and look at old pictures and movies, whereas I carry the experience with me. I will not see a movie twice. But, then again," he adds, "as I get older, I sometimes watch a movie a second time without realizing I saw it the first." ❧

The concentric arches in the auditorium were inspired
by similar structures at Radio City Music Hall and are accented by vents
that serve two purposes: to allow light to pass through and to provide ventilation,
heating, and air-conditioning, which was the original function
of those found at Radio City.

The
Gold Coast

HIGH STYLE ART DÉCO BLOSSOMS
BENEATH THE PALMS

The Gold Coast is precisely that—taking its name from

that horseshoe of platinum-white beaches that stretches north along

the western coast of Florida. It's the sort of place to which

the rich and celebrated flee from the rigors of civilization to lose

themselves among the truly civilized pursuits of fishing, boating,

and lounging beneath the breeze-fanned palmettos. But the theater,

though southerly in accent, can trace its beginnings to a muggy

Manhattan day in the middle 1970s. It was back then that

the theater's owner, Lloyd Wright—an attorney and namesake

of Frank Lloyd Wright—found himself in New York

between business meetings.

"I had a few hours to kill," he remembers, "so I decided to go see a movie. The picture was *2001: A Space Odyssey.* They had the film projected onto this enormous screen that wrapped around the auditorium. I thought to myself: 'This is how movies can compete with television. You've got to make it a bigger experience.' These days, they're making theaters smaller, and they're crazy. They should get big, wide screens that wrap around—get sound all over the place. Make it something the average person is never going to have in his home."

When, several decades later, Mr. Wright decided to add a theater to his Florida home, he heeded his own advice—for the Gold Coast is hardly average. And neither, for that matter, is

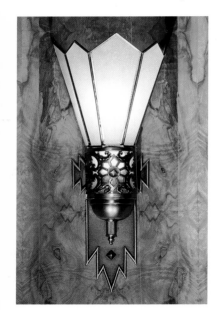

The Gold Coast's marquee entrance, paneled with bookended burlwood, boasts a neon and incandescent sign designed after that of the Riviera Theater in Charleston, South Carolina. The antique Art Déco sconces are solid-cast brass with frosted glass.

Mr. Wright. Although his hair is silvered and his face, seamed by sun, reminds one of a senator or dignitary, his conversation—which rambles as casually as a beachside stroll, then darts with sudden agility—obviates any such comparison. His conversation, in fact, is effortless—and enjoyable, as well, because his own pleasure is so delightfully contagious. A widower, retired from the practice of law, Wright regales visitors with tales of his travels, which are constant and not infrequently exotic. He has trekked through India on elephant-back, delved into the remotest regions of Africa, explored Antarctica, and traversed the Russian Steppes. Many of these adventures he has chronicled in

the local newspaper, whose *pro bono* travel editor he happens to be. "It's a wonderful job," he laughs. "Not only do you not get paid, but because I insist that the pictures I take be printed in color, they cost me about eighty-five bucks apiece to get them in there."

The coastal island where he has his winter home (another, larger house sprawls along the shore of Lake Ontario in Rochester, New York) is little more than an enlarged sandbar overgrown by tangles of tropical foliage. The homes are, for the most part, modest bungalows of the plantation sort, all meticulously insulated from one another by thick clouds of hibiscus and coconut groves. A road uncoils from one end of the island to the other along the beach, whose sea shines like blue milk-glass. The total year-round population is about 600, for as Mr. Wright points out, few inhabitants are natives: "When you come down, you discover nobody's grown up here," he jokes. "A few rednecks around town maybe. That's it."

Yet few rednecks can be seen. The island's resort hotel (owned by Mr. Wright) caters to tourists flown south from parts north, most of whom dress with self-consciously casual opulence, their sun-tanned faces and arms aglitter with gold—spectacles, watches, chains, bracelets, earrings, even gold teeth—suggesting a perfectly reasonable explanation for the region's 24-karat nickname. Those who are not guests of the hotel are college-age kids who have seasonal jobs or assorted part-time residents. The latter includes artists (such as Rauschenberg and Lichtenstein), socialites, and media personalities—most notably Ted Koppel, who happens to be Mr. Wright's newest neighbor. "He's on *Nightline*," explains Mr. Wright, who didn't recognize Koppel when they met. "I had to apologize. I said, 'I've never seen the show before.' He's on at 11:30 at night. I told him, 'You've got to come on earlier than that, because I'm in bed by then.'"

Wright's house sits on four acres that open onto the beach. The house—a Bermuda-style

The marquee doors, bearing stylized figures on double-sided etched glass, are replicas of those found in the 1929 Powhatan apartment building on South Chicago Beach Drive in Chicago. The mahogany pilasters are topped by capitals adapted from the La Mamounia Hotel in Marrakech and gilded in 24-karat gold leaf (a necessity in the humid Floridian climate). The sconces, found in the RKO Studios warehouse, date from the 1930s. The terrazzo floor's design is typical of the Déco period.

The marquee entrance and foyer together form an octagon,
so that the foyer spatially mirrors the entrance.
Extending from the outer marquee area, the pilaster and woodwork
motifs are carried out in the foyer as well. The foyer's settees
are upholstered in "Boris Kroll" fabric from Scalamandré.
The granite-topped bar functions as an entertainment
area for serving guests refreshments.

bungalow—was built in 1968, a closed, rather dark dwelling, "terribly depressing." There were no skylights, and the windows were small. So Mr. Wright brought his decorator down from New York and proceeded to remodel the home, opening up the space. "We knocked holes in the walls," he recalls, "and nothing is the same. I realized halfway through it would have been a helluva lot cheaper if I had just torn it all down and built a new house. But by that time, it was too late." The results, however, justify the effort and expense: the house, combining wood beams and pink, highly polished stone, has opened up, so that its interiors shimmer like the pearly surfaces of a Gulf conch.

Mr. Wright's ambitions for the house, from early on, called for a private theater. When he came across Kalomirakis' work in *Connoisseur* magazine, the possibilities intrigued him. He wrote Kalomirakis in care of the magazine, and the designer wrote back. It was at this point that both men enthusiastically embarked on a creative voyage that would last five years. The causes of this delay were several, the foremost being that local regulation forced them to scrap the original plan calling for an addition to the house. "We had to start over," explains Mr. Wright, "and that knocked a whole year off."

The second plan, however, worked out for the best. The theater is housed in a separate structure on the estate, one that was built specifically for it, allowing Kalomirakis to enlarge the floor plan. On entering the theater building (on top of which guest quarters were constructed), one finds oneself standing on a multicolored terrazzo floor before the Gold Coast box office. Inside, a voluptuous blond drags in ennui at her cigarette, while above, the neon bars and arches of the marquee flash excitedly. The richly paneled mahogany walls boast vintage posters under glass, as well as sconces discovered in the RKO Studios warehouse. The foyer, reached through frosted-glass doors, is semicircular in shape and boasts a polished-granite-topped bar. Between full-length photographs of Clark Gable and Gloria Swanson, steps ascend to the auditorium entrance, from which the visitor has a view of the screen above the rows of velvet-upholstered seats. The Déco styling pervades here, as elsewhere in the Gold Coast—a treatment that was inspired by theaters in Mr. Wright's hometown of Rochester: "One theater in particular that I remember," Mr. Wright recounts, "was called the Palace. When I talked to Theo, that's what I thought of. If I see a movie, I want to see it in a decent theater. I haven't been to a commercial theater in twenty years. I wanted something elegant from the late 1920s or early 1930s."

Elegance abounds in the Gold Coast, which is the nearest movie theater—commercial *or* private—for 40 miles. And for Mr. Wright and many of his friends, it offers a unique opportunity to experience their favorite films in a classic context. For Mr. Wright, whose lifestyle and tastes run to the extremes of quality and scale, this means drama, "scenery," as he calls it. "Give me marching Roman soldiers by the thousands. Give me Cleopatra, give me a travelogue. You need a little size in a film

The foyer displays a full-length studio portrait of Gloria Swanson, taken during the making of *Sunset Boulevard*. The proscenium—flanked by decorative, backlit Art Déco-style grilles—can be viewed through the mahogany-and-brass portholed doors of the foyer.

to justify a theater. Otherwise, you might as well show it on television. On the other hand," he adds after a pause, "people who are watching epics on their little 21-inch TVs are making a big mistake. They're missing out on a lot."

And Mr. Wright, you can be certain, misses out on nothing. ◆

The corrugated ceiling plays off the
illuminated side coves that line the length
of the auditorium. The wall, curtain, and chair
fabrics are by Scalamandré. The auditorium
sconces, also from RKO, are variations
by the same artist of those found
in the marquee entrance.

The
Bubble Hill

◆

No one, it seems, can explain why Bubble Hill is so named,

except perhaps its owner, who can be as elusive as the explanation.

One is reminded, in comic-book fashion, of the quest to discover the

meaning of the word "Rosebud" amid the lurid chiaroscuro

of twisted shadows and white glare in Orson Welles' *Citizen Kane*.

The curious, however, must in this case make their way

not to the precipitous Gothic perch of Xanadu, but to the

garden-strewn lane of a suburb not far from Manhattan.

Here, instead of an iron-spired gate bearing that ominous "K,"

one finds a neat section of low-bricked walls on which

is inscribed the enticing moniker, "Bubble Hill."

In the foyer (preceding page) hangs a gold- and silver-leaf Art Déco mirror, circa 1933. A softly lit view from the foyer includes the lobby (hung with portraits of Lena Horne and Sidney Poitier), the theater marquee, and the entrance to the auditorium.

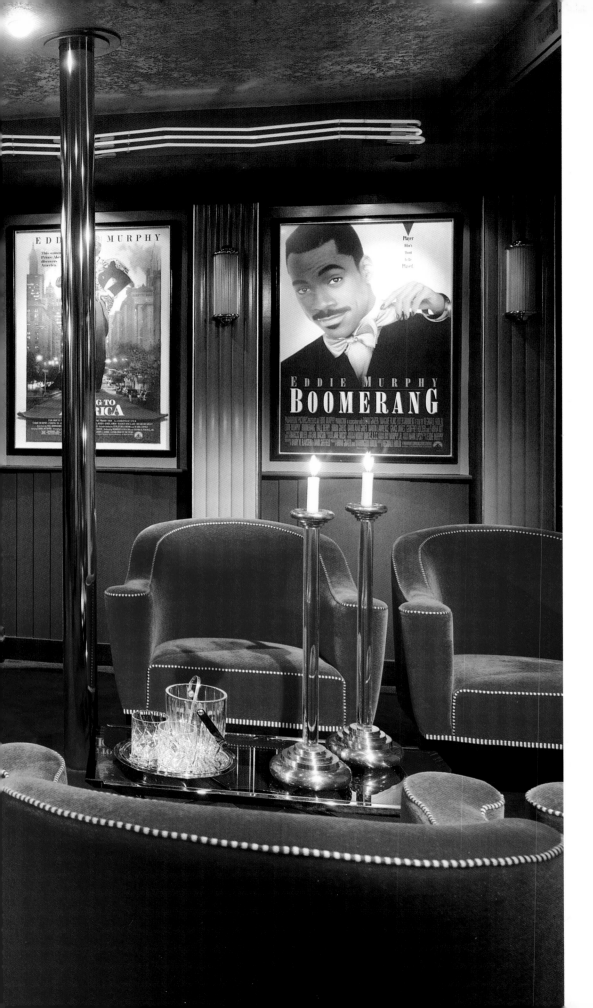

The gate is hardly forbidding; and indeed, the guard who periodically emerges to eye the ever-present bands of curious pilgrims merely smiles and shakes his head at their flash-cube antics. They are, after all, a part of the daily life at Bubble Hill: they are, as the property's owner says, something to be lived with.

The owner is actor Eddie Murphy, whose longest-running engagement thus far has been as husband and father of three. Murphy often retreats to this tranquil spot (family in tow), behind whose gates undulating lawns of velvet-clipped grass roll upward to lap at the stone steps of a colonnaded colonial house of indeterminate size. Within this well-protected domain, Murphy assumes the nocturnal routine that evidently suits him best, one in perfect harmony with his role as *Vampire in Brooklyn*'s creature of the urban night. His day begins at approximately four in the afternoon, when he rises, has breakfast, and spends some much-valued time with his children. Afterwards, he repairs to his studio, one of several separate buildings on the

The theater entrance, flanked by posters from many of Murphy's films, faces a fully functional refreshment area (not shown). The chairs arranged throughout the lobby were designed by Josef Hoffmann in 1913 and produced by Wittman, Austria.

property, where he practices his second art—recording music. (There is a third, as well, for he has been known on occasion to paint, studying his easel for hours. His mother, Mrs. Lynch, whose eyes cast an ironic gleam, remarks, "We thought he was going to be an artist. He was always drawing on easels as a child. Anyway, he did a lot of signing his name—on everything. I saw an easel come out two or three years ago, he set it up in his room and did a couple of things. I actually have a piece, and because he's famous, someone will call it art.")

In addition to the studio, where Murphy spends most of his time, Bubble Hill comprises a gym, a racquetball court, a bowling alley, a pool, and, of course, the theater, which takes its name from the estate. This seeming excess of utility is largely a function of his post-meridian lifestyle: formerly, after

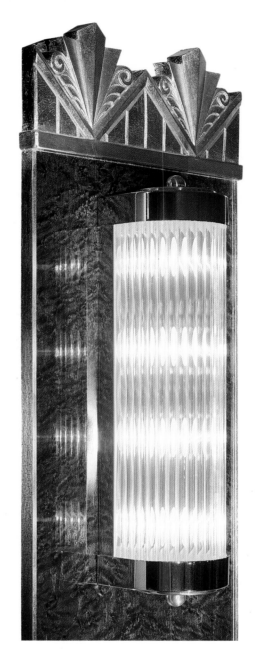

a long day on the set, if he wanted to bowl, he would go with friends to an all-night alley, working the lanes until two in the morning. Now, everything he used to go out for can be found somewhere at Bubble Hill. In fact, notes Mrs. Lynch, her grandchildren (the oldest of whom is six) don't go anywhere without someone in attendance; and surveying the battery of closed-circuit security screens near the kitchen, one perceives their wisdom in not wandering too far astray. Yet, despite its vastness, Bubble Hill has a strong, though eccentric, family spirit. Never far, but never notably near, the teasing laughter of children can be heard, accompanied now and then by a glimpse of a boy, presumably Murphy's son Miles, darting past outside in pursuit perhaps of the family's cocker spaniel. One earnestly believes Murphy's assertion that there is not

Sconces shown in the pilaster detail are by Boyd of New York.
The hand-polished bird's-eye capital atop the pilaster is leafed in two tones
of antique gold. In the theater proper, pilasters line walls upholstered
in Gainsborough velvet from Schumacher, which is also used for the screen
drapery. Chairs designed by Zographos Designs of New York are covered
in the "Radio City Marble" line of Schumacher fabric. The custom table
accommodates an AMX controller and video projector.

a part of his home he doesn't enjoy. And it says a great deal for the theater that, of all its many parts, this is his favorite.

Located in the basement, the theater is reached by a steep set of stairs carpeted, like the foyer below, in a deep burgundy. The space is softly lit by recessed ceiling lights and contemporary interpretations of Déco torchieres, whose glow, reflected in mirrored walls, glimmers over the curves of consoles and immaculate framed photographs. These are of himself on the set, of friends, admired artists. Two drawings on dinner napkins by Peter Max brighten one wall, while, on another, a few pictures of Elvis hang. (Here I am breaking a promise not to invoke Elvis: when Murphy once mentioned in an interview that he was a fan, a barrage of Presley paraphernalia descended, so much, in fact, that an Elvis Room

upstairs had to be dedicated to its storage.) There are framed posters of his own films—*Harlem Nights*, *The Golden Child*—beside the ticket booth, which remains conspicuously vacant: Murphy's wife, Nicole, is unnerved by the uncannily lifelike dummies ("When it's dark," says Mrs. Lynch, "they give her the creeps") that haunt other Kalomirakis creations.

The theater room is relatively intimate. Instead of the traditional folding seats, velvet armchairs and sofas furnish the space. Murphy did not want a particularly formal theater, given the time he spends here; moreover, his children, regular attendees at the Bubble Hill, can make themselves at home: sometimes, when their parents watch a film late, the children will curl up on the sofas and fall asleep.

In the tradition of many a Hollywood mogul, Murphy's theater, though equipped with laserdisc, as well as VHS, relies primarily on two 35mm projection machines to make its magic, owing largely to Murphy's ability to readily obtain prints of first-run films. He watches more movies, he says, than the average person, and although countless televisions punctuate the elegant prose of the house (Murphy is an admitted television addict), he also watches major broadcast events in the theater. Even so, each time he comes back here, it's a new experience.

Mrs. Lynch, who generally has all the answers to questions concerning the theater, does not, however, have the answer to the one question that remains—that of the name. She only remarks that the estate was christened while Murphy was still a bachelor, which leads one to speculate: does the name suggest a void to be filled—by a family, a wife? Or is it, rather, a wry acknowledgment that every reverie has its waking moment, that this bubble of perfect peace may someday, pricked by the demands of daily life, burst? Who can say? She knows only this: "Everybody loves the place. But I don't think anybody could love it more than Eddie does."

The
Cinema

AN ARCHITECTURAL AFTERTHOUGHT
TAKES CENTER STAGE

———◆———

*Y*ou would not think, to meet him, that Mr. John Marciano

was the sort of character capable of an afterthought,

much less acting on one. An investment broker in his thirties with

a benignly analytic gaze (a glance is sufficient to sum up one's

net worth) and an efficient, matter-of-fact manner, Mr. Marciano cuts

the classic figure of the brass-tacks businessman. This is not to say,

however, that there is anything in the least brassy or brusque about

him. Indeed, his quiet graciousness, in so subdued, so pensive,

a person, assumes an elaborateness of gesture that, at moments,

takes one off guard. This confluence of exactitude and the

desire to accommodate shows itself in his methodical,

exhaustive response to any question.

For instance, his explanation as to why the Cinema was not part of the original plan for his new Long Island house: "It is one of the things I regret," he says, "because, had I included a theater prior to construction, I would have built a bigger one—and maybe a bit of a different entrance to it. But because it was an afterthought, we had to deal with many structural obstacles, which required modifications. To make any further modifications would have been prohibitively expen-

sive. Still," he adds, somewhat soberly, "I'll tell you, if you survey people who have walked through the home and are impressed with its magnitude, eight out of ten will tell you they like the movie theater best."

To say so is saying a great deal, given the home in question. Set among the winding country roads of Long Island, the classi-cally styled Georgian home's clay-brick facade presides, from behind stone steps and white Corinthian columns, over an orderly cobbled courtyard. Inside and out, it reflects to perfec-tion the personality of its owner: serene, disciplined, composed, traditional. Straight lines contrast with subtle curves through-out, while various materials—oak paneling, alabaster, pastel marbles—create an assured atmosphere of permanence. Elegant

porcelain jars and gold-accented French Regency escritoires complement the architectural drama of the home, rather than interfere with the integrity of its progress. A formality exists throughout—even in the media-*cum*-family room; yet the spaces are refreshingly free of any element of stuffiness, and a welcoming nonchalance, a family vitality, suffuses these bright interiors. Young children are in scattered evidence: a doll lying upon a chair, a child-safety gate barring a flight of stairs. "When we first moved in," says Mr. Marciano as he passes this curiosity, as if by way of apology, "our son had never been around stairs before. So we were very concerned about all of the stairs in the house. But now these gates are unnecessary. He just climbs over them."

Stairs, however, are not the only attractions for Mr. Marciano's son, age two, and daugh-ter, age six. In the basement, where their playroom is located, for instance, there is a racquetball court, which also doubles for basketball: at the press of a button, a mechanized backboard descends from the ceiling on a steel cable. In addition, there is the theater, which was eventually created from a large rectan-gular space left empty by the architect—empty, that is, except for

In order to avoid a too-commercial flavor,
the Marcianos elected to use incandescent lights for the marquee sign,
rather than neon. Black polished granite reflects lights and images
in the gallery. The sconces flanking the corridor are mounted on pilasters
of dark-stained mahogany inlaid with light French walnut.
The stylized capitals are accented with gold leaf.

The lounge area in the main foyer faces the marquee entrance.
The cove ceiling—framed in dark-stained mahogany to match the pilasters—
gleams with 24-karat gold leaf that has been glazed over.
The fabrics covering both the bar stools and sofa
are from the "Boris Kroll" line by Scalamandré.

a large support column fixed at its center. "To get to their play room, the kids have to go through the theater, so it does lend itself to being a temptation," notes Mr. Marciano. "Had we thought about the theater when we first designed the house, we would have put it off to the side, so it didn't interfere with any other space."

This area presented several problems from the standpoint of coherent design. The placement of the column made a larger theater auditorium impossible. However, by subdividing the large room into a foyer, bar, and enclosed auditorium, Kalomirakis optimized the dimensions in which he had to work, maintaining the flow of traffic, which required that a corridor pass through one end of the theater area—the one leading to the children's playroom. "I've kept the theater off limits to the kids," says Mr. Marciano, disconcertedly eyeing a blonde, sun-dress-clad plastic figurine sprawled wantonly on the video console. "Which is why I am surprised to find a Barbie down here."

Of course, he doesn't mean that it's entirely off limits—some of the theater's features, after all, were incorporated with the young Marcianos specifically in mind. The proscenium beneath the stage, for example, enables the kids to put on shows of their own—something in which his daughter especially delights. Her father has even promised her a screening party for Disney's *Pocahontas*. But, as Mr. Marciano points out, the theater is primarily for his wife, himself, and their friends. "Before we had children," he says, "we went to the theater once a week. Having the children made it a little more difficult. It's pretty nice to be able to go in there and enjoy the theater ambiance that ordinarily we wouldn't have been able to have in our

family room or den. We'll have friends over—or family—for a movie or sporting event, a big fight, and we have a lot of fun."

By partitioning the area as he did, Kalomirakis devised a suite of rooms uniquely suited for entertaining. One enters through the aforementioned corridor, which serves as the theater exterior. Above the entrance doors, the sign's incandescent lights flare, while beyond them, bulbs flicker across the coffered ceiling. Lit by sconces, the foyer's inlaid pilasters frame full-length, life-size studio portraits of such film greats as the Little Rascals and Clark Gable. Brass-handled glass doors lead to the barroom, where a fully functioning bar faces vintage movie posters. The glazed, coved ceiling mirrors in gold leaf the milling audience below, as they gather before and after the show to sip a glass of champagne or talk together on the sofa.

To either side of the bar proper, portholed doors upholstered in leather lead into the theater auditorium. This area—like the foyer and bar—is patterned after no particular era or style. Traces of classical references are visible: the gilding on the column details, the coved ceiling, the grace of line. But, most noticeably in the choice of materials—the wood hues, the velvet, the warmth of the fabrics—the design is, at the same time, not distinguishably post-modern. This eclectic composition instead employs a vocabulary all its own—one that is neither embellished nor sparse, but that strikes a balance between the contemporary and the traditional, bringing this distinct space into aesthetic harmony with the remainder of the house.

"I didn't want a modern or chic type of theater, or anything like that," Mr. Marciano recounts. "On the other hand, I didn't want it to be so old and antique that it would look almost

Inspired by the loge doors of the Paris Opera, the doors to the theater auditorium are upholstered in leather with a trim of brass studs. Step lights guide guests up to the back row.

unusable, so we tried to find a cross between the two. I happen to like symmetry a whole lot; I like consistency in design, so I had Theo draw it for me. It's very, very usable and very, very comfortable, not stuffy, and I'm pleased with the way it came out."

Now that the Cinema is finished, Mr. Marciano—who, as he admits, had always considered private movie theaters to be the privilege of "those stars out in Beverly Hills"—relishes telling family, friends, and business associates about how the theater evolved. "It's a great piece just to talk about," he says. "It's almost like a work of art. I go through its history, how it started, what it became, and people are intrigued—by the quality of the work, by the photographs, by the marquee, and by the sound." Then—as an afterthought—he adds, "Really, by the whole thing, how it came together." ◈

A unifying element throughout the space, pilasters divide the auditorium into niches in which floating fabric panels conceal the acoustical insulation that helps to fine-tune the theater's sound. The sconces of solid brass and glass are by Boyd of New York. The ceiling stencil adds a subtle texture that echoes the fabric scheme of the foyer. The rocking chairs by Irwin Seating are upholstered in velvet.

The Savoy

ART DÉCO FOR AN ECLECTIC ECCENTRIC

◆

Sarah Winchester, the rifle heiress, was told by a fortuneteller,

after the sudden deaths of her husband and child, that the spirits

of all who had been killed with Winchester guns would avenge

themselves on her in the next world. This fortuneteller went on to

inform Mrs. Winchester that, if she began a project, say, a house,

and labored at it day and night, she would never die. Alas, poor

Sarah *did* pass on, but her immense, rambling, incoherent

Victorian house in San Jose, California, testifies to her

reluctance to make that final exit, bestowing on her

its own ironic brand of immortality.

F. Schumacher red velvet upholsters the walls of the foyer, whose carpet is a reproduction of the Donald Deskey design from the lobby of Radio City Music Hall. The sconces are original Sabino cast glass from the 1930s. Mahogany pilasters with gold-leaf capitals line the foyer, at the end of which presides an Art Déco bas-relief panel in silver leaf.

Mrs. Winchester's eccentricity appeals to Bill Jones, who is reminded of the Winchester house whenever he discusses his own Byzantine building project in Ormond Beach, Florida. A manufacturer from Brooklyn, New York, Mr. Jones and his wife, Jan, relocated their business to Florida many years back in order to escape the congestion of the city and to raise their three children in a somewhat more wholesome environment. The move entailed some risk: their business, at the time, had barely found its footing, and so the Jones family economized. This meant living in a 2,100-square-foot house crowded with kids, furniture, and the spoils of Mr. Jones' dual enthusiasms, history and collecting: 7,000 toy soldiers, an assortment of British Victorian "militaria," coins, stamps, comic books, movies. Thus, when the family began designing a new home that could accommodate these accumulations, they blended various architectural styles, as Mr. Jones notes, to keep everything in its proper perspective. "I'm kind of a frustrated architect in my own mind," he explains. "We designed this house kind of like an amusement park. Each room's got its own theme. We've got a 1950s room, a Hollywood-style bedroom, Art Nouveau, everything—you name it."

This ménage is encased within the bricked walls of a Gothic and Romanesque exterior, around which, somewhat surrealistically, a Floridian jungle swarms. To wander the halls is to cross barriers of time, to travel from ancient Egypt to an African rain forest; from a Victorian parlor to a 1930s night club suited to the likes of Myrna Loy and William Powell. In fact, fans of classic film, the Joneses often refer to themselves jokingly as the "Nick and Nora Charles of Ormond Beach."

Hence their choice of Art Déco as the proper style for their theater, which came to the blueprints somewhat belatedly.

The columns that accent the auditorium are inspired by those from the façade of Elysée-Palace Hotel, designed by Camille Garnier. The wall fabric is Frank Lloyd Wright, while the wainscoting is bird's-eye maple. Reproductions from George Hurrell negatives of Bogart and Garbo hang at the rear of the room.

The bronze-leaf grilles flanking the proscenium are
re-created from a pattern on the elevator doors of a 1930s building
at 275 Madison Avenue in New York City. The curtains are
F. Schumacher velvet with bullion fringe.

The original plans for the house only included a media room. When Mr. Jones discovered that they would require an enclosed space without windows for a true theater, he ordered the contractor, à la Winchester, to tear off the almost-completed roof and add another story.

One accesses the Savoy (which occupies this second floor) either by stairway or elevator. From its marquee entrance surfaced in polished black granite and burlwood to its upholstered foyer adorned with a silver-leaf bas-relief sculpture of Déco design, the Savoy is pure period—the ideal atmospheric accompaniment to Mr. Jones' favorite film, *The Maltese Falcon*. "I like that whole era, that whole black-and-white feeling," he says. "It's a feeling that something is going to happen. The Savoy is a place you go to be completely transported away. You never know what year it is until you walk outside."

To do so is to see, still, a work in progress. Although Mrs. Jones asserts, "It's time for the house to be done," Mr. Jones is not sure he wants it to be, for he envisions this as the sort of house that, like Sarah Winchester's, one hundred years from now, will remain a unique, if eccentric, creation. "Besides," he adds, "I wouldn't want the evil spirits to get me." ◆

The
Mayfair

———◆———

*P*ermanence, tradition: these qualities more than

any others characterize Mr. and Mrs. Arthur Goldberg,

whose house in the New Jersey countryside also serves as

home to the Mayfair. Despite the complex formula of their lives—

they are parents, grandparents, successful business people

(Mr. Goldberg is the president of Hilton Gaming),

political supporters (they regularly attend campaign fund-raisers

and can, on occasion, be glimpsed at a cocktail party given by,

say, Senator Ted Kennedy), and philanthropists (Mrs. Goldberg is

energetically immersed in projects aimed at revitalizing

downtown Newark)—their philosophy of living expresses

surprising fidelity to a single theme: family.

Certainly this is the *raison d'être* of their home, an American rendering in brick and stone of an English manor house that (its rather formally gabled and corniced facade notwithstanding), inside, leaves all stuffiness at the umbrella stand by the door. The generously proportioned rooms open one into the next, inviting the visitor to follow: it is the sort of place that lends itself as readily to a candle-lit, black-tie reception as to a wiener roast in one of the massive fireplaces on a winter's afternoon. For the warmer months, the property offers a pool, a hot tub, and even a waterfall; and its 22 acres of woods and fields are actually a working hay farm. The farmer, a woman, brings her own tractor during harvest time. "It's perfect," says Mrs. Goldberg. "She takes care of the hay, then leaves. She does the house next door as well, so it's really worked out nicely. And our furniture seems happy here. Everyone says, 'Oh, you must be building a smaller house now that your children have grown.' And I say, 'No, believe it or not, it's larger.' Because now that I have grandchildren, our last home just didn't work. Here, the rooms are set up differently. We can be in this house summer, winter, spring, and fall and still be happy. This house satisfies every season."

The family for whom Mr. and Mrs. Goldberg have labored began, appropriately enough, in a theater in Hillside, where they themselves first met. She was fifteen, he seventeen, and they would rendezvous there on Friday nights to watch (or not watch) movies with friends. Memories of that theater, the Mayfair, remain understandably close to them both, though this vintage cinema has, to their regret, been somewhat altered by time: "It's triple 'X' now," explains Mrs. Goldberg. "So you wouldn't want to be caught dead there." Which is why they decided to bring a small part of it home.

Initially it was Mr. Goldberg who championed the cause. Several years before, he'd happened across one of Kalomirakis' designs in an issue of *Architectural Digest* and mentioned to his wife that, if they should ever build a house, this was something he'd like to have. While the original plans called for a standard media room in the basement, Mr. Goldberg, recalling the article, pressed for something different. "He was the one who really encouraged this room," Mrs. Goldberg admits. "He was the one who wanted to see it done properly, to have all of the ambiance of a theater. It was one of the few rooms in the house that he specifically requested we do the way he wanted."

What Mr. Goldberg wanted was a classically styled theater that would make a bold aesthetic statement—not simply an assortment of padded chairs, special lights, and good equipment. When he met with Kalomirakis (whom Mrs. Goldberg tracked to his Brooklyn brownstone), he was excited by the vision they shared. That vision, translated from abstraction into wood, plaster, and gold leaf, has taken the shape of a classically European auditorium with pronounced Italianate overtones.

The ticket lobby's floor is a multicolored terrazzo design. The box office is constructed of two-toned solid mahogany with ebony pilasters and gold-leaf capitals. True to the style of the era, the sign is formed of incandescent lights, rather than neon. This long shot shows the enfilade of rooms leading from the ticket lobby and foyer to the orchestra foyer and the auditorium. The custom sign above the entrance reads, "Midnight shows on the roof garden every Saturday and Sunday."

One enters from a hallway that resembles a street corner: doors to one side lead into a pool hall; opposite, a wine-shop door opens on the wine cellar; and directly ahead, the Mayfair's ornately paneled ticket booth shelters the matronly ticket-seller (known to the family as "Elsie"), who languidly puffs a cigarette. Glass-encased posters line the exterior of brickwork and limestone, while above, streams of bulbs blaze across the marquee. Mayfair guests enter by crossing the paneled lobby, hung with film portraits and bathed in the frosted glow of a period chandelier.

Beyond, the auditorium presents a sculptural spectacle of texture and color. Arcades of semicircular arches line three walls, the recesses of which are upholstered in a lush burgundy brocade woven with thread of gold. The coffered ceiling, richly hued in burgundy, gray, and 24-karat gold leaf, is set with intricate medallions that conceal recessed spotlights. The seats, also brocaded, descend in tiers to the proscenium, where the

Beside the solid mahogany ticket booth, the incandescent marquee lights top the walls of the ticket lobby, which are made of brick pilasters and carved limestone panels. The working poster displays are framed in mahogany.

screen hangs behind thick velvet curtains. These elements of Old World opulence conjure a setting worthy of the most venerable palazzo, a sensitivity of taste to impress even the most discriminating merchant prince. Indeed, a neighbor— one of the first acquaintances to view the completed Mayfair—was so impressed, that he could not resist promptly phoning a business associate to describe the experience. Shortly afterward, Mr. and Mrs. Goldberg received a call from Donald Trump: their neighbor, Trump complained, had barely batted an eye the first time he visited Mar-a-Lago, but he couldn't say enough about this theater. What, Trump wanted to know, did *they* have that was so wonderful? Mr. and Mrs. Goldberg graciously invited him over to find out for himself.

In the foyer, the wall panels are upholstered with Scalamandré silk fabric. The trimmings, moldings, and doors are solid mahogany. The ceiling fixture dates from 1920 and was recovered from a theater in San Francisco. The ceiling itself is glazed, while the surrounding frieze is Lincrusta (an embossed wall covering) highlighted with gold leaf. The photographs— original studio portraits from the 1930s and late 1940s—are of Jean Harlow, Fred Astaire, and Susan Hayward.

One of the Mayfair's most charming (and telling) features is the paved walk that approaches the ticket booth. Inlaid with multiple shades of faux granite, this "Walk of Fame" bears stars for each member of the family—with room, naturally, to add on. This design evolved from a proposal Mrs. Goldberg had made to the board of directors of New Jersey's Performing Arts Center, of which she is a member: she had suggested a star walk for the center made up of the names of entertainers born in New Jersey; the idea eventually inspired this treatment in her own theater. "Because it's done in Hollywood," she observes, "it puts you in a theatrical mode the moment you cross it. And I thought:

'What better way of doing this than to have our family members as the stars?' Because they truly are. That's the reason I'm building this house."

Mr. and Mrs. Goldberg, both movie fans (the Humphrey Bogart of *African Queen* and *Casablanca* is a favorite), can now watch films whenever they like—and *how* they like. This hasn't always been possible, since the commercial theaters in the area are typical of the claustrophobic boxes with which most of us must contend. "We saw *The Postman* last night at one of these very small theaters here," Mrs. Goldberg remarks. "And we kept thinking we'd like to see it on a big screen with big

sound. Our theater has wonderful sound, and that makes a big difference when you're watching a movie—being able to hear it properly."

In the Mayfair, the Goldbergs can hear and watch their movies properly together, surrounded by their favorite stars—their family. And although their Mayfair is much grander in style, if not in dimension, than the original movie house that, as teenagers, they used to visit on Friday nights, still, there in the dark, each time the curtain rises, their memories flicker like firelight across the silver screen. ◄►

A subtle color scheme emanates from the panel fabric in the alcoves that line the theater auditorium, providing a chromatic focal point that complements the pilasters. The Scalamandré fabric is the same that was used to upholster the Pope's throne for the last U.S. papal visit. Matching fabric can be seen on the theater's seats and curtain. The moldings and ceiling incorporate motifs in green, dusty rose, and beige pastels, accented with 24-karat gold leaf. Dedicated light sources dramatically illuminate the Romanesque system of ceiling vaults and pilasters with silk-screen inlays.

The
Loews Pitkin

THE GEOMETRY OF PAST AND PRESENT
REFLECTED IN A FINITE SPACE

———————————◆———————————

The Loews Pitkin, for all its streamlined elegance,

was essentially designed by fax. The proprietors, Mr. and Mrs.

Arnold Simon—owners of Bill Blass and Calvin Klein, whose sultry,

slinky blue-jeans advertisements with their denim curves grace

billboards from Seattle to Syracuse—travel perpetually on business,

and their schedules left little time for firsthand supervision of their

home's construction, though this certainly did not prevent them

from becoming deeply involved. Quite the contrary, as Mrs. Simon

notes, the home—situated on several lushly wooded, pleasantly

cultivated acres within commuting distance from Manhattan's

concrete wilderness—is the splendidly material manifestation

of the dream she and her husband shared.

"This is the first time we have ever built a home of this magnitude," she says. "Life has definitely changed for us over the years. We're self-made, and we've become very successful. My husband and I wanted to experience building our own home, incorporating his dreams and my dreams all into one, and seeing what we came up with."

The result was a cream-colored French Renaissance château with, here and there, a Mediterranean accent, an openness to soften the formal edges. The ceilings are lofty, the windows large and bright, looking onto sun-drenched leaves and pools of blue shade. The house has two wings, but despite its immensity, the rich mélange of Clarence House and Scalamandré fabrics, there is a connectedness, so that one wouldn't feel in the least awkward lingering with friends around the center island in the French Provincial kitchen over a bottle of Bordeaux. It is a home to suit the lifestyle of its owners, one that revolves around family and entertaining. Though they've enjoyed phenomenal success, they're both fairly young and extremely creative. "We go to clubs," explains Mrs. Simon. "We work in the garment center. We're fun people. So our house is very homey, but eclectic. And because we entertain a lot, it's a party house, too."

The theater, located on the lower level, embodies each facet of their lifestyle—at once an incomparable entertainment area for urbane party guests and a family retreat for Mr. and Mrs. Simon and their three children. Neither contemporary, nor specifically period, the space quite literally reflects the mood of the given moment. Entering from a staircase, one encounters the theater's marquee in a blaze of incandescent lights and neon bars, which spark along the outer terrazzo floor like bursts of fireworks across the surface of a lake. The marquee walls are of vitrolite, an unusual treatment very popular in the Déco period consisting of a lacquered glass that provides a dazzling high-gloss finish. The panels, in tones of warm gray, are separated by strips of satin brass. The box office, also covered in vitrolite, shelters an elderly woman holding tickets. (She is unique among the figures pictured in this book, because she is not soft-sculpture, but ceramic, the work of artist Gary Mirabelle.) Poster cases containing vintage titles flank the box office on all sides, while the rectangular pattern of the terrazzo floor mirrors the geometric motif of the marquee's coffered ceiling.

Through the solid mahogany doors, one enters a foyer, past which aisles (also paved with a geometric terrazzo) encircle the theater auditorium in a horseshoe pattern separated from it by a series of columns. These columns provide support for the upper floors of the house and had to be incorporated into the design. Kalomirakis solved this problem by establishing the surrounding aisle space, which allows the audience to circulate around the central theatrical area, and he even furnished a small lounge

The Loews Pitkin marquee entrance revives the Art Déco technique of paneling walls with vitrolite, which consists of clear glass panels lacquered on the reverse side and separated by strips of brass. Ruby red and aqua neon stripe the marquee sign bearing the theater's name, which is taken from a movie house in Brooklyn. The box office is flanked by display cases of brass-framed glass that can be opened to change the posters. The floor of the marquee entrance by Amtico echoes that found in the lobby of the RCA building in Rockefeller Center, whose symmetrical lines typify the streamlined 1930s American idiom and complement the coffered ceiling studded with incandescent bulbs.

with console table and benches in the far corner. This spatial layering is visually enriched by the choice of materials and lighting. The color scheme inside, for example, is much darker than in the outer areas, lending depth. Further dramatizing the multi-dimensional effect, custom-designed rectangular light panels frame the arches between the columns, as well as the columns themselves. Reminiscent of Frank Lloyd Wright, the light casings are sliced stone-colored mica set in satin brass containing, in total, one and a half miles of strip lighting. Their geometric glow is multiplied to infinity in the black-mirrored panels that line the outer walls of the theater: one is immersed in the world of illusion, as though one stood in a hall of mirrors—all sense of context is lost once inside. There is an eerie thrill to the experience, as one seems to glimpse a lustrous fusion of time and space in which past and present become one.

For Mr. Simon, this is the perfect balance. An inveterate moviegoer as a child, he has vivid memories of the old theaters that populated his Brooklyn neighborhood—the Paramount,

the Carol. In fact, the Loews Pitkin is named for one of these. "It was very old," he recalls, "even then. It was a big theater, and I remember that the ceiling had stars in it, and the decor was a very old style—sort of red velvet and gold leaf." But, although he has always wanted a movie theater of his own (his schedule seldom allows him time for public theaters), he and his wife decided not to replicate that style. "We're recapturing the experience," he explains. "We're not recapturing the look. My wife wanted Theo to do whatever he wanted."

Mrs. Simon, who deals with Calvin Klein's artists and designers daily, firmly believes in letting talent pursue its natural course: "When you find talent, you let talent go, and that's how I run my business. I like Theo's feel, his personality, his depth for theater design. Who am I to dictate to him what to do? If he ever came to me and told me, 'I'm going to design Calvin Klein jeans,' I'd throw him out the door. But when it came to the theater, I said, 'Theo, do whatever you want.' And he'd say, 'Well, I want you to see it.' 'Okay,' I'd tell him, 'fax me

The entrance foyer contains a lacquered Art Déco console by Jóia accented with a Tiffany crystal vase. The two benches are by Sandringham, Ltd., and are upholstered in Schumacher fabric. The pictures of Clark Gable and Jean Harlowe are prints from original negatives at the MGM archives. The inner foyer (opposite) offers similar seating beside another lacquered Art Déco table. Six studio portraits hang along the walls.

a picture.' And he would, and really that's how we did it. Occasionally he'd come over and show me some color schemes and so forth, but we basically did a lot of things by fax."

This philosophy of artistic indulgence has paid off in a room of really rare beauty and vision, proving Mrs. Simon's gift for enabling creative individuals to achieve unique depths of expression. "I wanted something that I could be proud of, something very special that no one else had. And so I just let Theo's mind go. Thank God," she says sighing contentedly, "for faxes." ◈

Audience members do not enter directly into the auditorium; instead, they experience the theater gradually, framed between arches—a plan inspired by the layout of Grauman's Chinese Theater in Hollywood. A series of columns and pilasters compose the background for a system of rectangular arches that lines the pergola-like horseshoe of the theater's outer aisles, which surround the auditorium proper. These rectangular arches are illuminated by geometric panels made of brass and clad with sheets of mica. The walls are covered with black-mirrored panels that reflect the lighted arches, creating the effect of a hall of mirrors. In the background can be seen the refreshment stand, while the theater auditorium (right) can be glimpsed through the arch.

Designed by James Rosen and made by Pace Gallery, New York,
the Fumo Lounge Chair was chosen for the theater's seating.
The upholstery is Schumacher fabric. The carpet,
"Lineal Weave," is by Bentley.

The proscenium arch is also framed by illuminated mica panels.
The curtains are of red velvet. The bullion fringing the curtains
is custom-designed by Scalamandré.

CREDITS

The Ziegfeld

Contractor Joe Di Staulo
Foreman Hank Hansen
Painter Bill Gianella
Electrician Van Natta Electric
Lighting Consultant Tom Drew
Millwork Frank Pollaro
Metal Fabrication Artistic Fabrication
Moldings The Decorators Supply Corp.
Theater Seating Irwin Seating
Foyer Furniture Brueton, Dakota Jackson
Fabrics Craig Fabrics, F. Schumacher & Co.
Carpeting F. Schumacher & Co.
Wall Upholstery General Drapery Services
Foyer Flooring Classic Marble
Entrance Sign Drama Lighting
Antiques Artisan Antiques
Light Fixtures Boyd, Krell Lighting
Posters Lou Valentino
Poster Restoration Garo
Ticket Booth Sculpture Lisa Lichtenfels

Audio Visual Designer Eric Eidelman
Installation Company Audio Video Interiors Ltd.
Products ADA, AMX, Boston Acoustics, ESE, Furman, JBL, Linetouch, Pioneer, Sony

The Paramount

Contractor Brad Carlson
Foreman Fred Mergenthaller, Gary Zoller
Painter Ciro De Grezia
Electrician Shock Electric
Acoustical Consultant Keith Yates
Millwork Woodwise
Metal Fabrication Excalibur
Fiberglass Fabrication
    Warner Brothers Staff Shop
Sculptor Troy Nelson
Moldings The Decorators Supply Corp.,
    Flex Moulding Inc.
Theater Seating Irwin Seating
Foyer Furniture Sandringham Ltd.
Fabrics Brunswick & Fils, Old Weavers,
    Scalamandré
Trimmings Scalamandré
Carpeting Stark Carpet
Wall Upholstery Eastern Decorators
Stage Curtain Eastern Decorators
Entrance Flooring Magnan D. & Co.
Foyer Flooring Woodwise
Entrance Sign Accurate Signs
Graphics Manhattan Signs & Design
Antiques Gallery 63, Lost City Arts
Light Fixtures Dave's Lamps, Excalibur,
    Urban Archeology
Light Fixture Restoration Dave's Lamps
Posters Lou Valentino
Poster Restoration Garo
Foyer Photos Lou Valentino
Ticket Booth Sculpture Lisa Lichtenfels

Audio Visual Designer Eric Eidelman
Installation Company Audio Video Interiors Ltd.
Products ADA, AmPro, AMX, Apogee Sound,
    AST, AudioEase, Autopatch, AVI, Bose,
    Bryston, Chaparral, Crest, Denon, Faroudja,
    Fiber Options, HD Visions, JBL, JVC,
    Linear-X, Marantz, Mitsubishi, Oxmoor,
    Pioneer, Rane, Runco, Sonance, Sony,
    Stebelton, Wurlitzer

The Uptown

Contractor Bob Eustic
Painter Rick Hickson
Electrician Mark Ferris
Lighting Consultant Paula Dinkle
Acoustical Consultant Keith Yates

Plaster Fabrication Warner Brothers Staff Shop
Fiberglass Fabrication
    Warner Brothers Staff Shop
Theater Seating Irwin Seating
Fabrics F. Schumacher & Co.
Trimmings F. Schumacher & Co.
Carpeting F. Schumacher & Co.
Wall Upholstery Stan Lusk
Stage Curtain S&K Theatrical Draperies
Entrance Sign Nite Life Neon
Antiques Lost City Arts
Light Fixtures Aamsco Lighting,
    Artisan Antiques
Posters Lou Valentino
Poster Restoration Garo
Foyer Photos Lou Valentino
Ticket Booth Sculpture Lisa Lichtenfels

Audio Visual Designer Robert Eitel
Installation Company
    Robert's Home Audio & Video
Products AudioEase, Bogan, JBL, KEF,
    Magician, Media, Mitsubishi, Nakamichi,
    Pioneer, Sonance, THX

The Apollo

Contractor DeWitt Construction
Project Manager Phil Therhorst
Painter Terry Hunt
Electrician Bob Bahr
Millwork Custom Woodwork
Theater Seating Rolf Benz
Fabrics Scalamandré
Trimmings F. Schumacher & Co.
Carpeting Hokason
Wall Upholstery Custom Walls, Inc.
Entrance Sign Finé Neon
Posters Lou Valentino

Poster Restoration Garo
Foyer Photos Lou Valentino

Audio Visual Designer Bill Anderson
Installation Company Genesis Audio Video
Products AMX, Audio Quest, Faroudja,
  Mitsubishi, Rane, Runco, Snell, Stewart
  Filmscreen, Triad

The Copper Beach

Contractors Mike and Don Cappy
Foreman Fred Mergenthaller,
  Gary Zoller
Painter Ciro De Grezia
Electrician Doug Melishar
Fiberglass Fabrication
  Warner Brothers Staff Shop
Moldings Flex Moulding Inc.
Theater Seating Irwin Seating
Foyer Furniture Pat Motilinsky
Fabrics F. Schumacher & Co.
Carpeting Bentley
Wall Upholstery Eastern Decorators
Stage Curtain Eastern Decorators
Entrance Sign Accurate Signs
Antiques Artisan Antiques
Light Fixtures Krell Lighting
Posters Lou Valentino
Poster Restoration Garo

Audio Visual Designer Brett Sandgren
Installation Company Audio Command Systems
Products Adcom, B&W, Creston, Middle
  Atlantic, Mitsubishi, Pioneer, RCA, Sony,
  Stewart, Velodyne

The Gold Coast

Contractor George Parker
Project Manager Dudley Curtis
Electrician Charlie Curn
Millwork Rail Guthrie, Bradley Rockwood
Glass Fabrication Alpat Stained Glass Studio
Plaster Fabrication Renaissance and Technology
Laser Cutting Laser Machining
Moldings The Decorators Supply Corp.
Theater Seating Irwin Seating
Foyer Furniture Design America
Fabrics Scalamandré, F. Schumacher & Co.

Trimmings Scalamandré
Carpeting Bentley
Wall Upholstery Dudley Curtis
Entrance Flooring Amtico
Entrance Sign Accurate Signs
Graphics Manhattan Signs & Design
Antiques Lost City Arts
Light Fixture Restoration Dave's Lamps
Posters Lou Valentino
Poster Restoration Garo
Foyer Photos Lou Valentino
Ticket Booth Sculpture Lisa Lichtenfels

Audio Visual Designer Eric Eidelman
Installation Company Audio Video Interiors Ltd.
Products AMX, Beldin, Boston Acoustics, JBL,
  NEC, Pioneer, Radia, Sonance, Sony, Stewart

The Bubble Hill

Contractor Joe Di Staulo
Foreman Steve Hanko
Painter Bill Gianells
Electrician Northern Valley Electric
Millwork Frank Pollaro
Metal Fabrication Artistic Fabrication
Glass Fabrication Galaxy Glass & Marble
Dolby Sound Consultant Bob Warren
Moldings The Decorators Supply Corp.
Theater Seating Zographos Design
Foyer Furniture Brueton, Wittmann Austria
Fabrics F. Schumacher & Co.
Trimmings F. Schumacher & Co.

Wall Upholstery Eastern Decorators
Stage Curtain Dobesch Associates
Entrance Sign Accurate Signs
Antiques Artisan Antiques
Light Fixtures Boyd, Artemide
Foyer Photos Lou Valentino

Audio Visual Designer Eric Eidelman
Installation Company Audio Video Interiors Ltd.
Products ADA, BTX, Christie, Comprehensive,
  Dolby, Essany, Extron, Faroudja, ISCO,
  JBL, Kelmar, Mogami, Neumade, Pioneer,
  Simplex, Sony, Speco, Strong

The Cinema

Contractor Peter M. Avedon
Construction Coordinator Vincent Catala
Decorator Donna Avedon
Painter Ciro De Grezia
Electrician Michael DeMeo
Millwork Woodwise
Theater Seating Irwin Seating
Foyer Furniture Nicoletti, Sandringham Ltd.
Fabrics Scalamandré, F. Schumacher & Co.
Trimmings Scalamandré
Carpeting Bentley
Wall Upholstery Eastern Decorators
Stage Curtain Eastern Decorators
Entrance Sign Accurate Signs
Light Fixtures Boyd, Krell Lighting
Posters Lou Valentino
Poster Restoration Garo
Foyer Photos Lou Valentino

Audio Visual Designer Robert Kaufman
Installation Company Audio Command Systems
Products Creston, Faroudja, JBL, Knox,
  Mitsubishi, Pioneer, Sony, Stewart, THX

The Savoy

Contractor Bob Weinberg Custom Builders
Project Manager Leo Towsley
Electrician Courteaux Electric Co.
Painters Steve Harper, Ludlow Lambertson
Millwork Steve Keefer, Tim Hamilton,
  Bill Christenson
Custom Hardware Klaus Wagner
Custom Capitals Troy Nelson

Theater Seating Irwin Seating
Fabrics F. Schumacher & Co.
Trimmings F. Schumacher & Co.
Carpeting F. Schumacher & Co.
Wall Upholstery Eastern Decorators
Entrance Sign Altec Sign Group
Posters Lou Valentino

Audio Visual Designer Rick Barnes
Installation Company Stereotypes
Products Creston, Draper, McIntosh, Runco

The Mayfair

Contractor Rick Nerdling
Foreman Eric Gaardsmoe
Painter Bill Blaine, Matt Moylen
Electrician Brett Wyatt
Millwork Woodwise
Silk Screening George Wittman
Moldings The Decorators Supply Corp.,
    Flex Moulding Inc.
Theater Seating Irwin Seating
Fabrics Scalamandré, F. Schumacher & Co.
Trimmings Scalamandré
Carpeting Bentley
Wall Upholstery Eastern Decorators
Stage Curtain Eastern Decorators
Entrance Flooring Amtico
Entrance Sign Accurate Signs
Graphics Manhattan Signs & Design
Antiques Lost City Arts
Light Fixtures Dave's Lamps, Krell Lighting,
    Urban Archeology
Posters Lou Valentino
Poster Restoration Garo
Foyer Photos Lou Valentino
Foyer Photo Reproduction Color By Pergament
Ticket Booth Sculptures Lisa Lichtenfels

Audio Visual Designer Robert Kaufman
Installation Company Audio Command Systems
Products Audio Command, Boston Acoustics,
    Bryston, Clarion, Creston, Denon, Draper,
    Pioneer, Rane, Sony, Triad

The Loews Pitkin

Contractor Tony Bruzzesi
Foreman Roy Pallarino

Painter Wojciech Ziebowicz
Electrician Fred Santaite Jr.
Millwork Woodwise
Metal Fabrication Jay Gibson Design
Glass Fabrication Galaxy Glass & Marble
Theater Seating Pace Gallery
Foyer Furniture Joia, Sandringham Ltd.
Fabrics Scalamandré, F. Schumacher & Co.
Trimmings Scalamandré
Carpeting Bentley
Wall Upholstery Eastern Decorators
Stage Curtain Eastern Decorators
Entrance Flooring Amtico
Entrance Sign Accurate Signs
Graphics Manhattan Signs & Design
Light Fixtures Dave's Lamps, Krell Lighting,
    Urban Archeology
Posters Lou Valentino
Poster Restoration Garo
Foyer Photos Lou Valentino
Ticket Booth Sculpture Gary Mirabelle

Audio Visual Designer Eric Eidelman
Installation Company Audio Video Interiors Ltd.
Products ADA, ADC, AMX, Apogee Sound,
    Crest, Extron, Faroudja, Foray, JBL,
    Litetouch, Oxmoor, Pioneer, Sierra, Sony

The Royal

Audio Video Installation Pierre Spenard
Contractor Paul LeFrance
Metal Fabrication Excalibur

Moldings The Decorators Supply Corp.,
    Sommerset
Theater Seating Quinette
Fabrics Scalamandré
Trimmings Scalamandré
Carpeting Bentley
Entrance Sign Hightech Applications
Foyer Photos Lou Valentino

The Roxy

Audio Video Installation Lance Braithwaite,
    Mike Percoco, Bob Warren
Architects Alvarado, Thrun, Maeda
Contractor Steve Spyrou
Electrician Mike Chrisicopoulos
Light Consultants Daniel R. Lotten,
    Phillip A. Evola
Theater Seating Irwin Seating
Carpeting F. Schumacher & Co.
Stage Curtain Harry Zarin
Entrance Signs Mercury Neon
Posters Lou Valentino

The Loews Grand

Audio Video Installation Bob Serio
Painter Renaissance
Electrician Michael Curry
Moldings Crown Corporation, The Decorators
    Supply Corp.
Theater Seating Irwin Seating
Fabrics F. Schumacher & Co.
Trimmings F. Schumacher & Co.
Stage Curtain General Drapery Services
Entrance Sign Drama Lighting
Light Fixtures Krell Lighting, Peerless
Posters Lou Valentino
Poster Restoration Garo
Foyer Photos Lou Valentino

The Bijou

Audio Video Installation Robert Eitel
Contractor Matt Kehoe
Project Manager Frank Gallagher
Millwork Don Cox
Glass Fabrication Frank Gallagher
Theater Seating Theater Design Associates
Fabrics F. Schumacher & Co.
Carpeting Hokason
Wall Upholstery Custom Walls, Inc.

Photography

All photography by Phillip H. Ennis, except as noted
on the following pages:

Page 2: Scala/Art Resource, N.Y.
Page 4: Corbis-Bettmann
Page 5: Erich Lessing/Art Resource, N.Y.
Pages 6–7: Robert Polidori/Planet
Page 8: The John & Mable Ringling Museum of Art
Page 9, bottom: Everett Collection
Page 9, top right: UPI/Corbis-Bettmann
Pages 12–13: Carl Iri Photography
Page 14: UPI/Bettmann Newsphotos
Pages 16–17: D.R. Goff/CAPA
Page 17, bottom: UPI/Bettmann

Designer: Michele Locatelli
Design Director: Ken deBie
Creative Director: Robert Ross
Text: Sabon $^{10}/_{20}$
Display: Kuenstler and Didot
Electronic Pre-Press and Color Separation: Digital Color, San Diego
Printer: Mandarin Offset, Washington, D.C.